Why Japan Can't Reform

Also by Susan Carpenter

SPECIAL CORPORATIONS AND THE BUREAUCRACY: Why Japan Can't Reform

Why Japan Can't Reform

Inside the System

Susan Carpenter
The University of Edinburgh Business School, UK.

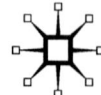

First published 2008 by
PALGRAVE MACMILLAN

Palgrave Macmillan in the UK is an imprint of Macmillan Publishers Limited, registered in England, company number 785998, of Houndmills, Basingstoke, Hampshire RG21 6XS.

Palgrave Macmillan in the US is a division of St Martin's Press LLC, 175 Fifth Avenue, New York, NY 10010.

Palgrave Macmillan is the global academic imprint of the above companies and has companies and representatives throughout the world.

Palgrave® and Macmillan® are registered trademarks in the United States, the United Kingdom, Europe and other countries.

ISBN-13: 978–0–230–22070–6 hardback
ISBN-10: 0–230–22070–3   hardback

This book is printed on paper suitable for recycling and made from fully managed and sustained forest sources. Logging, pulping and manufacturing processes are expected to conform to the environmental regulations of the country of origin.

A catalogue record for this book is available from the British Library.

Library of Congress Cataloging-in-Publication Data

Carpenter, Susan, 1943–
    Why Japan can't reform : inside the system / Susan Carpenter.
        p. cm.
    Includes bibliographical references and index.
    ISBN 978–0–230–22070–6 (alk. paper)
      1. Japan – Economic conditions – 1989– 2. Industrial policy – Japan.
    3. Government business enterprises – Japan. 4. Corporations,
    Government – Japan. 5. Structural adjustment (Economic policy) –
    Japan. I. Title.

HD4313.C353 2008
338.952—dc22   2008029960

10 9 8 7 6 5 4 3 2 1
17 16 15 14 13 12 11 10 09 08

Printed and bound in Great Britain by
CPI Antony Rowe, Chippenham and Eastbourne

To the Japan Policy Research Institute (JPRI)

Contents

Part II   Inside the System

Foreword

Business fads and fashions come and go, but Japan's rise and fall from grace as an industrial model is a particularly remarkable demonstration of the fickleness of opinion about economic and business affairs. In the early 1980s, the world woke up to Japan's remarkable post-war success story, and the floodgates opened. Research and publications on the reasons for the success of Japan's major companies poured out.

At the start of the 1990s, the bubble burst and Japan slid into a decade-long recession, from which it has, on many measures, still not recovered. Advocates of the Anglo-American model of capitalism were quick to assert its superiority, and publications such as Porter and colleagues' *Can Japan Compete?* were soon emerging. The 1997 economic crisis in Asia further reinforced the trend. In the debate about the superiority of different varieties of capitalism, Asia was a goal or two down.

Since then, the perceptions of the state of Japan and its economy on the part of many outside of Japan have not improved significantly, although Japanese companies continue to dominate many world markets. In 2007, Japan's difficulties in achieving the political consensus to drive through reforms received coverage across the world. Susan Carpenter's analysis of reform in Japan is therefore timely. The book contains a wealth of information and anecdotes about various attempts to achieve structural reform in Japan, and gives readers fascinating insights into why this has been such a slow, painful and, in Carpenter's view, ultimately unsuccessful exercise.

The book demonstrates how the social cohesion that can be so useful in some contexts can equally easily manifest itself as collusion on the part of ruling elites. Sadly for the reformers, and no doubt to the relief of those who support the status quo, Carpenter's analysis suggests that there is little prospect for light at the end of this particular tunnel.

Nick Oliver
University of Edinburgh

Acknowledgements

I would like to express my deep appreciation to Professor Nick Oliver for recognizing the significance of the book and to Professor Jonathan Crook for encouraging me to write a second book.

I would also like to thank Professor Paul Thompson for his support of the initial effort in 2003.

Acronyms and Abbreviations

BOJ	Bank of Japan
BP	Basic Pension
CPI	Consumer Price Index
DBJ	Development Bank of Japan
DPJ	Democratic Party of Japan
EPI	Employees' Pension Insurance
FAZ	Foreign Access Zone
FDI	Foreign Direct Investment
FILP	Fiscal Investment and Loan Program
GATT	General Agreement on Tariffs and Trade
GDP	Gross domestic product
IAI	Independent Administrative Institution
IBJ	Industrial Bank of Japan
IRCJ	Industrial Revitalization Corporation of Japan
JDP	Japan Development Bank
JETRO	Japan External Trade Organization
JFTC	Japan Fair Trade Commission
JH	Japan Highway Corporation
JMPA	Japan Magazine Publishers Association
JNEPA	Japan Newspaper Editors and Publishers Association
JNOC	Japan National Oil Corporation
JPRI	Japan Policy Research Institute
LDP	Liberal Democratic Party of Japan
LTCB	Long-Term Credit Bank
MAC	Ministry of Agriculture and Commerce
MCI	Ministry of Commerce
METI	Ministry of Economy and Industry (formerly MITI)
MITI	Ministry of International Trade and Industry
MOF	Ministry of Finance
NCB	Nippon Credit Bank
NHK	Japan Broadcasting Company
NPL	Non-Performing Loans
NTT	Japan Telephone and Telegraph

OECD	Organization for Economic Cooperation and Development
SCAP	Supreme Commander of the Allied Powers
TIRB	Temporary Industrial Rationalization Bureau
SCAP	Supreme Commander of the Allied Powers
SIA	Social Insurance Agency
SMEs	Small and Medium-Size Firms
WASP	White Anglo-Saxon Protestant
USTR	United States Trade Representative
WTO	World Trade Organization

Part I

The System

1
Introduction

> Elite officials may have lost the ability to run an advanced
> industrial economy, but they continue to be masters of
> creating a façade of change. Perhaps no regime in the world
> history has been as accomplished in the use of diversionary
> tactics to deflect pressure for a fundamental realignment of
> power.
>
> (Mikuni and Murphy, 2002)[1]

In 2003 the author published *Special Corporations and the
Bureaucracy: Why Japan Can't Reform*.[2] The book concerns the
public corporations that were established by Japan's national
ministries in the 1950s and 1960s to aid in the restoration of
Japan's war-devastated economy. It was the first book in English
that focused on these organizations as the vehicles during Japan's
post-war years that have served to perpetuate a rigid and ingrown
system of government administration of the political economy,
which can no longer accommodate the pressures of a rapidly changing social political economy.[3] Indeed, Special Corporations are at
the heart of government administration because they effectively
are extensions of the national ministries. Furthermore, the corporations, along with their subsidiaries, have come to serve as the
route which ministry officials can use to migrate to upper-management positions in private industry after their retirement from
their agencies.

Until the late 1990s there were few books in Japanese regarding
this subject. It may seem surprising that very little was written about

3

them prior to this time, but the paucity of literature is related to several factors:

1. Until the Law Concerning Access to Information Held by Administrative Organs was enacted in 1999 there was a minimum of information regarding how public corporations operated in terms of annual expenditure, how the corporations used their budgets, and the sources of the funds.[4] In other words, operations were concealed from public scrutiny. The information available to the public is still scanty because the organizations are not required to reveal how they receive funds other than tax revenue. Also, accounting systems used by public corporations differ from private corporations.
2. The efforts of academics and journalists to access comprehensive and reliable data about Japan's political economy is complicated by the insularity of organizations and their reticence to open their doors to either Japanese or non-Japanese observers.[5] The Japanese social political system is relatively opaque compared to Western industrialized nations, and gaining a solid understanding of a given environment can be difficult and time-consuming. This is particularly true of ministerial operations, because the ministries are very protective of their territory and control the flow of information tightly. Mikuni and Murphy related in their book *Japan's Policy Trap* that scholars and analysts find that accessing reliable data concerning bureaucratic policies is problematic because there are no records of court cases, debates, or hearings.[6]

Nevertheless, since the early 1990s as Japan's recessive economy continued unabated, public demand for structural reform of the public sector saw a significant increase of books and articles by Japanese commentators and politicians calling for the dissolution of public corporations because they advanced the vested interests of the ministries as well as an obsolete civil service system.

Special Corporations (*tokushuhojin*) are types of large public corporations supported primarily by large corporate funding from the Postal Accounts Agency, the state-run banking system and the Financial Investment Loan Program (FILP), often referred to as

Japan's secondary budget. FILP was established in 1953 as a big financial conglomerate operated in the public sector. The largest part is postal savings and another part is the public pension fund.[7]

The government has had difficulty defining the exact characteristics of Special Corporations other than that they have assisted the government in promoting national interests. Nevertheless, they can be viewed as being corporations based on a national law, which has been approved by the National Diet. Special Corporations were established according to special establishing procedures through a special law, the Law of Establishment Act, Article 4–11 subject to the Ministry of General Affairs (renamed in 2001 the Ministry of Public Management, Home Affairs, Posts and Telecommunications). The law was neither civil nor corporate.

The corporations were established after the Second World War to aid in the reconstruction of infrastructure destroyed during the war to resuscitate Japan's industry. The corporations are linked to the industrial sectors under the administrative jurisdiction of each ministry. For example, the former Ministry of Construction (renamed in 2001 the Ministry of Land, Infrastructure and Transport) established the Japan Highway Corporation in 1956 to award contracts to construction companies to rebuild highway networks.

The Ministry of International Trade and Industry (MITI) (renamed the Ministry of Economy, Trade and Industry or METI in 2001) established the Japan Finance Corporation for Small Business in 1955 to give long-term, low-interest loans to small businesses. The Ministry of Finance established the Japan Development Bank (JDP) in 1953 to aid in Japan's economic recovery. Special Corporations that have international recognition are giant organizations such as the Japan Broadcasting Company (NHK) and the now partially privatized Japan Telephone and Telegraph (NTT).

Throughout the post-war era numerous subsidiaries ('children corporations') and subsidiaries of these subsidiaries ('grandchildren corporations') were established by ministry officials. Special Corporations, their 'children' and 'grandchildren' corporations and branch offices of Special Corporations effectively serve to place officials from the national ministries throughout Japan. The branches of subsidiaries can also provide posts for local government officials as well.

Chartered Corporations

Chartered Corporations are another type of large public corporation that are managed at the national level, such as the Central Bank of Japan (BOJ), the Japan Red Cross and the Chamber of Commerce and Industry. Unlike Special Corporations, Chartered Corporations were not subject to evaluation by the Cabinet or the National Diet. Before 1970, Japanese connected to private industry established Chartered Corporations with consent from the ministries. However, from 1968 onwards, the ministries began to establish such corporations at their discretion (namely by ministerial ordinance), and by 1978 there were 99 Chartered Corporations.

Window of opportunity for structural reforms

In 1992, the recession and the acknowledged need for action to ignite Japan's lagging economy triggered a struggle for power among factions in the Liberal Democratic Party (LDP), the party that had controlled Japan's post-war National Diet. Some disillusioned members defected to form two new progressive parties. Besides reform of the electoral system in 1994, reform of the public sector also was initiated, which included the dissolution of a few insolvent Special Corporations. By 1999, the number had decreased from 96 to 84 corporations, which had received ¥256 billion in subsidies from the National Treasury. But despite the decrease in numbers, by 2000 the amount of subsidies rose to ¥258 billion. In 2001 the government granted subsidies to Special and Chartered Corporations, totalling a whopping ¥5 trillion ($42 billion). This sum did not include loans from FILP or Postal Savings. Also, due to losses incurred, the government had to invest another ¥11 trillion.

When Koizumi Juniichiro assumed the office of prime minister in April 2001 there were 163 Special and Chartered Corporations remaining. A ultra-conservative career politician and the president of the Liberal Democrats (LDP), the party that has controlled the Japanese Diet since 1955 (with the exception of 1992–96), Koizumi's top priority was to deal with non-performing loans and to reform the finance sector.

In order to cut public spending that had climbed to 130 per cent of annual GDP in 2001, increasing to 140 per cent the following year,

Koizumi's platform also focused on reform of the state sector. The reforms included the downsizing of FILP, the privatization of the Postal Account Agency, the reform of the Social Security system, and cutting government funding to Special Corporations by one- third or ¥1 trillion ($8.3 billion). In an effort to streamline the bureaucracy, he intended to reform 109 of the 163 Special and Chartered Corporations through the integration of insolvent with solvent corporations, through privatization or through dissolution.

Another objective of the Prime Minister's reform measures was to strengthen the executive office by weakening the bureaucracy, the most powerful arm of Japan's government. The dissolution of Special Corporations would effectively block one of the main routes through which retired bureaucrats migrate to upper-management positions in private industry, allowing the bureaucracy more influence over the economy and, as importantly, over the executive office.

In name only

In 2003, 32 Special Corporations were renamed Independently Administrative Institutions (*dokuritsu gyosei kiko*) or IAI to signal that some reforms were being initiated. Koizumi's government devised a scheme that converted 38 of the Special Corporations and Chartered Corporations, whose numbers by 2001 had decreased to 87, through dissolution, privatization or consolidation, into IAIs with the expectation that eventually, financing from tax revenues would no longer be necessary. Similar to the 'law for the establishment of Special Corporations', the Incorporated Administrative Law, which was implemented on 13 December 2002 for the establish ment of independently administrative institutions, is neither a civil nor a corporate law.

The Ministry of Public Management, Home Affairs and Telecommunications released an explanation in English that outlines the concept of the new IAI system:

> The IAI System lies on the basic concept of public welfare, transparency, and autonomy of activities as Article 3 of the Law of the general Rules provides that (i) the IAIs must make efforts for just and effective operation under the consideration that the fulfilment of their undertakings is indispensable to people's lives, society

and the economy; (ii) the IAIs must make efforts to open to the public the status of their organizations and the operations by such means as the announcement of the content of their activities as provided under this law: (iii) the autonomy of each law must be respected in accordance with the application of the Law and the laws establishing the IAIs.

Although the number of Special Corporations has been reduced from 77 to around 53, there has been, so far, no evidence that Koizumi's plans have proven successful. More significantly, the reforms have not served to cut public funds to IAIs nor have they served to inhibit the migration of retired civil servants to the private sector since these corporations have subsidiaries. A survey conducted by the Lower House in 2007 revealed that ¥4.89 trillion in subsidies was provided to these entities and 27,882 former bureaucrats from the central ministries and agencies were working at 4576 public-interest and government affiliated corporations.

Known as *amakudari* ('descent from heaven'), the scheme is a part of the civil service system and under the jurisdiction of the National Personnel Agency. *Amakudari* refers to the practice of bureaucrats taking post-retirement positions in public and private corporations. The retired officials receive full salaries from their new organizations along with their civil service pensions.

The National Public Service Law stipulates that bureaucrats cannot, for a period of two years, legally move directly to positions in private companies attached to the sectors their ministries regulate. However, they can move immediately to Special Corporations, other types of public corporations, industrial associations or research institutes supported by their ministries, where they linger for two years on salary before going on to the private sector. It should be noted that tenure in public corporations does not serve to inhibit contact between retired civil servants and the private sector.

Why reform?

Japanese commentators take the perspective that the duties the government assigned to public corporations in the 1950s and 1960s, such as the allocation of funds for contracts for public works projects, the issuance of long-term, low-interest rate loans to small and medium-size businesses and low-interest rate mortgages should be done directly by the government or private institutions. They express particular concern that Special Corporations also breed subsidiaries which can provide post-retirement positions for civil servants and act as the main vehicles facilitating the smooth entry of civil servants into the private sector, thus perpetuating the link between business and government, and that they are the key mechanisms that serve to bind the political and economic system together, thus preventing structural reform.

In October 2001, the strongest opposition party, the Democratic Party of Japan (DPJ), together with the Socialist Party and the Free Party, called not only for sweeping reforms of *amakudari* in both public and private corporations, but also for restrictions on retired civil servants becoming members of corporate advisory boards.

Iishi Koki, a member of the DPJ who held a seat in the House of Representatives of the National Diet, was assassinated by a right-wing sympathizer in Tokyo on 25 October 2001. Iishi, whose concerns centred on political and administrative misconduct, contended that Special Corporations and other types of public corporations should be the focal point of structural reforms. In 1999, Iishi published a book about *amakudari* entitled *Bureaucratic Heaven: The Bankrupting of Japan (KanryoTenkoku Nihon Hassan)*. He followed this in 2001 with a book on public corporations entitled *The Parasites That Are Gobbling Up Japan: Dismantle All Special Corporations and Public Corporations! (Nihon wo Kuitsuku Kisiechu Tokushu Hojin Koeki Hojin wo Zenhaiseiyo!)*.[8] He claimed that the 76 Special Corporations in operation in 1999 had 2000 subsidiaries. Although his book may appear to be an effort by his party to weaken the bureaucracy and loosen the ministries' ties with the LDP, his report posed pertinent questions concerning the rapid escalation of public corporations that have been established through Special Corporations and government agencies, and the employment opportunities they offered to elite bureaucrats.

Iishi maintained that before structural reforms could progress, Special Corporations and public corporations must be dismantled. He believed that there had been little movement towards reform of any kind. The reluctance of the ministries to reform these corporations, thereby preserving their territory, symbolized the rigidity of Japan's political economic system.

Maintaining territory

Ironically, the reform of Special Corporations, including the migration of officials to Special Corporations, is being administrated by the ministries, the very agencies that are determined to maintain their corporations.

By 1972, Japan had achieved a 10 per cent annual GDP to become the world's third largest economy in the world (following the United States and the Soviet Union) and, realistically, many of the Special Corporations were no longer needed to support economic development and should have been dismantled. However, the ministries had come to rely on their corporations, because not only did they provide post-retirement positions for officials, but they also served to extend ministerial powers and increase administrative jurisdiction (namely 'territory'). The connections established between the ministries' officials posted in Special Corporations, their subsidiaries and their branch offices throughout Japan effectively link the ministries to the private sector. Additionally, through their officials posted at branches of Special Corporations and their subsidiaries, the national ministries can monitor local government policies and guide the planning of local policies.

Japan's foreign direct investment and the implications of *amakudari*

Japan's post-war economic development was supported by mercantile policies and protectionist measures that successfully limited foreign competition with domestic industries. However, Japan was fully industrialized by the late 1960s and the continuation of policies that frustrated foreign businesses entry into domestic markets also served to hinder the development of a domestic market and created a society that was heavily reliant on the state for subsidisation of both industry and the public sector, resulting in government debt that has climbed to approximately 180 per cent of annual GDP[9], the highest of the 30 members in the Organization of Economic Cooperation and Development (OECD). Mikuni and Murphy stated:

> In the past decade, Japan has appeared to have emerged as today's paradigmatic example of the ultimate bankruptcy of mercantile policies.
>
> (2002)[10]

Figures released by the OECD in 2006 reveal that Japan has the lowest rate of inward investment of the members of the Organization For Economic Cooperation and Development.[11] Government statistics released in September 2007 showed that direct investment was 3 per cent of the annual gross domestic product or ¥15.4 trillion ($144.8 billion). It recommends further deregulation of markets and the reduction of entry barriers to service and agricultural industries.

All governments protect domestic markets through the levy of tariffs and through regulations known as non-tariffs, but in Japan, as well as in those economies that are nurtured by government through protectionist industrial policies, there are invisible barriers to foreign direct investment and these are the most difficult to deal with because they can be the consequence of interpersonal networks between domestic business and government. Japan's civil service system effectively provides domestic industry with a convenient method of lobbying ministries that administrate their sectors. Companies are encouraged to hire retired elite civil servants, thereby forging effective pipelines with the ministries that administrate their sectors and lobbying their interests effectively through these officials. Since retired ministry officials receive retirement benefits from their agencies, they retain a sense of loyalty to their former colleagues.

In his book *Troubled Times*, Edward J. Lincoln agreed:

> The *amakudari* system provides substantial reason to be sceptical of the extent of deregulation and the unilateral market opening in Japan because of the manner in which this practice establishes a broad web of personal ties between government and Japanese firms.
>
> (1999).[12]

Amid the concerns of foreign investors about Japan's current economic environment and about the reticence of the ministries to further deregulate markets, in January 2008 Prime Minister Fukuda Yasuo promised that reforms would continue. Japan's Council on Economic and Fiscal Policy also advised in January that reforms in the tax system and regulations and more transparency in regulatory procedures were necessary to encourage inward investment. The Council also advised more bilateral free-trade agreements between the United States and the EU.[13] In 2006, Foreign Direct Investment

(FDI) in the United States and South Korea was 13.5 per cent and 8.8 per cent respectively. The recommendations were announced on 31 January, the same day that Japan's biggest banks announced that the losses incurred from the US subprime mortgage crisis had topped ¥529.1 billion.[14]

The image of reform

During Japan's post-war history, elite civil servants have been given powers to administrate Japan's economic development. Mikuni and Murphy published *Japan's Policy Trap* in 2002, analysing the reasons for Japan's continuing recessive economy and the inability of the government to pursue extensive structural reforms. Tracing elite rule back a thousand years to when an aristocracy governed Japan, they stated that elite bureaucrats are today's policy makers, operating independently of legal sanctions and thus enjoying unlimited power.[15] Indeed, prior to 1867 and the overthrow of the military regime that had ruled Japan since 1603 (known as the Tokugawa Era), marking the end of feudalism, the Japanese had relied consistently on an emperor or a military regime to govern them. Even after the fall of the military, a new power took its place – namely a bureaucracy.

During Prime Minister Hashimoto Ryutaru's coalition government administration from 1996–2001, there was an effort to reform the national ministries by merging some of the ministries and integrating some of the minor agencies into the ministries, while making some of the agencies that previously had been connected to the ministries independent agencies. However, the mergers did little more than change the names of various ministries. As an example, since January 2001 the Ministry of Construction has merged with the Ministry of Transport, the National Land Agency and the Hokkaido Development Agency to form the Ministry of Land, Infrastructure and Transport. Prior to the merger, the Ministry of Transport had managed 849 public corporations. The Ministry of Education, which operated 1811 public corporations, merged with the Science and Technology Agency to form the Ministry of Education, Culture, Sports, Science and Technology. The Ministry of Home Affairs merged with the Ministry of Management and Coordination and the Ministry of Posts and Telecommunications to form the Ministry of Public Management, Home Affairs, Posts and

Telecommunications. As noted before, the Ministry of International Trade and Industry (MITI) underwent a name-change. MITI is now known as METI or the Ministry of Economy, Trade and Industry to signify that the ministry is now planning policies for regional economic development.

The following examples illustrate the Executive Office's struggle to wrest territory (e.g., power) from the ministries through the downsizing of Special Corporations, the vehicles that perpetuate the *amakudari* system, encourage the contact between ministry officials and business, and promote the central bureaucracy's control over the planning of local government policies.

The image of reform: privatization of the Japan Highway Corporation

Koizumi first planned to abolish within five years the Japan Highway Corporation (JH), the Japan National Oil Corporation (JNOC), the Housing Loan Corporation and the Urban Development Corporation. These corporations were chosen for initial reform efforts because the organizations were debt-ridden due to the gross mismanagement of public funds.

The JH was established in 1956 by the former Ministry of Construction to handle and manage the construction of highways networks throughout Japan. Its president, vice-president and directors were traditionally elite retired officials from the Ministry of Construction who received retirement allowances while they served in the JH (the usual practice for civil servants who assume posts in public corporations). It had over 60 subsidiaries throughout Japan. FILP supplied the major funding. In theory, the JH repaid FILP loans with revenue collected from highway tolls, but these tolls were not enough to repay the loans. In Japan the highway and bridge tolls can be more expensive than bus and ferry fares and many commuters opt to use public transport.

Furthermore, since the JH distributed contracts to the construction companies, bid-rigging which involved large construction companies was commonplace. On 29 September 2005, the Fair Trade Commission ordered 45 Japanese steel bridge builders to cease the bid-rigging of bids for contracts from government and from the JH. The FTC alleged that 20 former officials in the JH, including former Vice-President Uchida Michio and a former executive board member Kaneko Tsuneo, had received jobs in 45 companies due to their engagement in the bid-rigging. Among the 45 firms named were Mitsubishi Heavy Industries Ltd., Ishikawajima-Harima Heavy Industries Co. and Kawasaki Heavy Industries Ltd. The FTC announced that the contracts procured through illegal bid-rigging were worth approximately ¥260 billion. Former JH officials who were employed in the bridge construction companies had accessed unpublished information in the JH regarding toll road bridge construction projects.[16]

Consequently, Uchida, and Kaneko, along with officials from 26 corporations and ten of their officials, were indicted on 8 December 2005 for bid-rigging. Some of the officials had been officers in the JH before their employment in the corporations. Besides the companies listed above, other corporations accused of bid-rigging included Mitsui Engineering and Shipbuilding Co., Sumitomo Heavy Industries Ltd, Hitachi Zosen Corporation and Nippon Steel Corporation Uchida and Kaneko were charged with instructing subordinates to carve up contracts for an elevated highway bridge in Shizuoka Prefecture in May 2004. The contracts inflated the JH's costs by ¥47.8 million. Uchida was arrested on 25 July 2005 and later fired from his position as vice-president of the JH on 22 August. Kaneko was arrested on 1 August.[17]

On 17 December 2005, they entered a plea of not guilty to charges, but the corporations pleaded guilty.[18] On 7 December 2007, Kaneko was found guilty of violating the Anti-Monopoly Law and sentenced to a two-year prison term. But it was suspended for three years.[19] At the time of writing, Uchida's trial is still in progress.

Koizumi had originally planned to privatize the JH by fiscal 2005 through the consolidation of three other debt-ridden public corporations – the Hanshin Expressway Corporation, the Metropolitan Expressway Corporation and the Shikoku-Honshu Bridge Authority, which carried massive debts. In total, the accumulated debt of these entities was ¥40 trillion. He intended that the single entity would repay the outstanding loan within 30 years. He also wanted to stop 40 per cent of future highway construction since the government spent ¥300 billion annually on highway construction. But the vested interests of LDP lawmakers, who relied heavily on contributions from their constituencies, who depended on public works projects for contracts and employment, and the bureaucrats, who relied upon post-retirement positions in construction-related businesses, opposed Koizumi's objectives. Koizumi's administration was pressured to produce a watered-down version of the original package that Koizumi was determined to get through the National Diet.

The original bill called for the repayment of the debt within 45 years, but the diluted version only focused on the completion of a 9342 km expressway, courtesy of a proposal from the Ministry of Land, Infrastructure and Transport. The costs are estimated to be ¥20.6 trillion. The repayment of the debt is doubtful. Two of the five-member advisory panel, who Koizumi appointed to review the reform and who had prioritized repayment of the debt, resigned on 23 December 2003 in protest, accusing the prime minister of failing to keep his promise. They stated that the new version of the bill contradicted the purposes of the original bill, which favoured repayment of debt over construction. But the revised bill would permit the continuation of state involvement in wasteful road construction and delay debt repayment.[20]

The last president of the JH was Fujii Haruho who was dismissed by the Land Minister Ishihara Nobuteru[21] after a highly publicized heated confrontation with Ishihara, who accused him of not cooperating in the process of privatization. Fujii assumed the post in 2000 after retiring as Vice-Minister of the Ministry of Construction. During the period he was in both offices, Fujii was popular among LDP politicians because he had expanded highway networks considerably and because of his close relationship with road construction firms.

The four public corporations were privatized on 1 October 2005. But instead of one entity, there are three; East Nippon Expressway Co. Ltd. (NEXCO East Japan), Central Nippon Expressway Co. Ltd. (NEXCO Central Japan) and West Expressway Co. Ltd. (Nexco West Japan). Nevertheless, the Ministry of Land, Infrastructure and Transport still engages in the management of highway networks.[22]

On 14 April 2004, Ishihara replaced Fujii with a LDP colleague, Kondo Takeshi, who was a member of the House of Councillors. Kondo had previously been an executive of Itochu Corporation, a major trading firm. Other directors appointed by Koizumi were former senior executives from Nippon Steel Corporation, Kobe Steel Ltd., Sumitomo Trust & Banking Co. and Tokio Marine & Nichido Fire Insurance Co. Kondo, who retired in April 2006, was succeeded by Yano Hironori, who was a former CEO of Toshiba Europe and a director at *Keidanren* (Japan Federation of Economic Organizations).

The image of reform: dissolution of the Japan National Oil Corporation

The privatization of the Japan National Oil Corporation (JNOC) is a second example of the determination of the ministries to maintain their corporations. METI's initial plans to dismantle the corporations were ambiguous regarding the sections to be liquidated and the sections to be sold, as well as the issue of *amakudari* in the organization.

The Japan National Oil Corporation was established in 1967 by the Ministry of International Industry and Trade (now METI) for the purposes of oil exploration and mining. The Japanese must import 99 per cent of their fossil fuel. METI oversees the energy-producing industries, among them oil. The ministry controls its imports and exports and refining through federations of oil importers. These federations connect METI to the oil refiners, who distribute to retailers. The domestic companies cooperate with foreign oil companies to engage in exploration, production and refining of crude oil, with foreign firms usually holding the larger share of the investment. JNOC had 142 affiliates and in August 2003 declared a net loss of ¥154.2 billion for fiscal 2002 and an accumulated debt of ¥770.1 billion due to the failure of its subsidiary, the Japan Oil Development Co.[23]

Traditionally, the president had been an elite official from the ministry, while retired officials from MOF filled other top management positions such as vice-president or director of finance. One of the major complaints lodged against the JNOC was that MITI officials took temporary positions for two years and forged relationships with both foreign and domestic companies, which led to permanent post-retirement positions in these companies.

Although JNOC was abolished, a major entity, Indonesia Petroleum Exploration (INPEX), that was established in 1966, merged with Teikoku Oil in March 2006 to form INPEX Holding Inc. The government owns 36 per cent. METI continues to be involved in operations even though it stresses that the company is partially private.[24]

The image of reform: *amakudari*

METI agreed to the discontinuation of *amakudari* in JNOC, but only if the system was allowed to continue in the Japan External Trade Organization (JETRO), a METI Special Corporation. It was a coup for METI since JETRO's operations had been receiving negative press in Japan and in the United States about its operations since 1995. JETRO maintains 73 offices in 54 countries and 36 branches in Japan. The corporation employs 830 staff in its domestic offices and 860 staff in its foreign branches.

JETRO was originally established in 1956 by the Ministry of International Trade and Industry to function as a promoter of Japanese small business exports, but has come to function as a vehicle that increases the territory, and consequently, the power of the establishing ministry. By 1972, the Japanese economy ranked as the third largest in the world behind the United States and the Soviet Union. By 1975, JETRO was operating 24 trade centres and 54 offices in 55 countries, testimony to the fact that not only had Japan become a major player in world markets, but also that MITI was planting roots overseas. Besides the JETRO offices, MITI officers were also posted to Japanese consulates, embassies and Japan Chamber of Commerce offices (a Chartered Corporation established by MITI) located around the world.

MITI used the JETRO offices as listening posts, keeping track of foreign trade regulations, foreign and domestic policies that would affect the import of Japanese goods, industrial and environmental standards, and government patent applications in anticipation that new inventions could be applicable for Japanese businesses. JETRO staff also collected macroeconomic data and surveyed foreign markets on behalf of Japanese businesses.

By the early 1980s, Japan, whose economy was export-driven, was showing a marked trade surplus with its trading partners, namely the United States, and there was significant pressure from the American government to deregulate domestic markets and raise import quotas for such goods as agriculture, electronic, motor vehicles and car parts. Realistically, JETRO's role as a promoter of Japanese exports was no longer as relevant to Japanese businesses as it had been in the 1960s and 1970s. Also, JETRO's role as a surveyor of foreign markets and a collector of economic and political data had, in part, become extraneous, because such research was being conducted by large Japanese multinationals and research institutes and by MITI commercial officers posted in embassies and branches of the Chamber of Commerce and Industry.

However, MITI was determined to continue operating an organization that had effectively resulted in creating more territory and more jobs for its officials. As a gesture of compliance with US demands to open markets, MITI began the process of re-orchestrating JETRO's functions so that the organization would serve as a promoter of foreign imports and foreign investment, a function which JETRO continues to provide. Nevertheless, the Japanese press in January, June and July 1995 took JETRO to task for no longer serving its original function. The *Asahi News*, a major daily, claimed that the ministries were changing the objectives of their organizations by contriving new roles. The newspaper called this 'skill at disguising' (*henshin no gijutsu*), pointing to JETRO as an example of a Special Corporation that had been established in 1956 for the purpose of promoting Japanese exports, but which now promotes imports.[25] The *Sankei News*, an ultra-conservative major daily, contended that JETRO was an underground MITI and that, in fact, it had become the Number Two Ministry of Foreign Affairs.[26] The monthly political magazine *Sentaku*[27] claimed that the CIA and FBI were keeping the directors of industrial research (METI) in JETRO New York under surveillance when they visited other JETRO offices in the US because they were suspected of industrial espionage.[28]

In the 16 June issue of *U.S. News and World Report*, William J. Holstein continued to probe JETRO's authenticity as an import promoter. He contended that JETRO America did not serve to promote imports into Japan, but rather was a sophisticated commercial intelligence-gathering agency. He suggested that the promotional materials served to disguise the true reason for JETRO's presence. In the article, Holstein quoted Edward Lincoln: 'At best the Japanese are being disingenuous when they say that JETRO's primary job is promoting American exports.' Lincoln also stated that JETRO's 'core mission' was to collect American technology and political intelligence.[29]

At a press conference on 22 November 2002, Cabinet State Minister of Administrative and Regulatory Reform Ishihara Nobuteru announced that he would like Diet members to realize that the continuation of Special Corporations was problematic and that a detailed review was necessary. Pointing to JETRO as an example, Ishihara said that he as well as the Minister if Trade and Industry were astonished to learn that the organization was advertising import promotion. Ishihara was implying that the importation of foreign goods should no longer be a primary concern because of Japan's recession and the contraction of the domestic market.

Although JETRO became an IAI on 1 October 2003, METI continues to operate the corporation and a retired METI official is the president. JETRO remains the primary government-supported organization that promotes imports and foreign direct investment. Nevertheless, as was previously stated, Japan's inward investment still ranks the lowest of the industrialized countries at 3 per cent of annual GDP.

Koizumi's legacy: privatization of Japan Post

Koizumi's pet project was the privatization of Japan Post, a government-run corporation offering postal and package delivery services, banking services and life insurance. It is the nation's largest employer with 400,000 employees (one-third of all government workers) and a nationwide network of 27,700 post offices.

The Postal Accounts Agency, the banking division of the Postal Service, is the world's largest bank. The state-run bank is the world's largest postal savings system as well as the world's largest holder of personal savings. Many Japanese prefer to put their savings into Postal Savings because the agency offers slightly higher interest rates than do private banks. They also feel more secure because government manages the institution. The bank manages 25 per cent of Japan's personal assets with ¥230 trillion ($1.7 trillion) in savings deposits and ¥120 trillion ($1.3 trillion) in insurance. The privatization of the agency will make it the world's largest commercial bank, outstripping Citigroup ($2.22 trillion) and Mitsubishi UFJ ($1.76 trillion).[30]

The government uses the Postal Accounts to fund public works projects, to provide long-term, low-interest-rate loans to small and medium-size firms, to offer long-term, low-interest mortgages and so forth. The funds are distributed through the Special Corporations.

FILP is partially funded by the Postal Accounts. The collection agency is the Ministry of Public Management, Home Affairs, Posts and Telecommunications. The dispersing agency is the Ministry of

Finance. However, Japan Post also holds ¥140 trillion in debt through government bonds. Koizumi contended that a privatized Japan Post would serve to curb government spending and the growth of public debt. The proponents of privatization claimed that privatization would help to eliminate a large source of corruption and pork-barrel patronage as well as allow greater efficiency and flexibility in the use of company funds.

But Koizumi's reform efforts met with stiff opposition, including members of his own political party, the Liberal Democrats. MPs rely on the postal office's significant resources to fund the public works projects. Many of the MPs' constituencies in rural regions were concerned about reduced services and loss of jobs. The rural postmasters traditionally have collected substantial funds from depositors in the postal Accounts for MPs' campaign coffers and have drummed up support for LDP candidates.

Koizumi's bill was initially voted down in the upper house of the National Diet in August 2005. Determined to get the bill passed, the prime minister dissolved the more powerful Lower House and called for a snap election. As the president of the LDP, he also kicked out 13 members of his party, who were opposed to the privatization, and successfully persuaded friends in the private and public sectors who were popular in the media to run for the election.

Nationwide elections for the House of Representatives were held on 11 September and Koizumi won the election with a majority. One of Koizumi's newcomers was Horie Takafumi, the flamboyant entrepreneur and president of the Internet portal operator Livedoor. Although Horie ran as an independent in the Hiroshima Sixth District, he received full support from the LDP. Horie lost the September election and his fortunes continued to decline when he was arrested on 23 January 2006 for securities fraud. He was released the following April on bail but after a lengthy trial beginning in September, he was convicted and sentenced to two and a half years in prison on 17 March 2007.

The privatization bill was passed in October 2005. Two years later in October 2007, the Postal Service was divided into four firms – mail, savings, insurance and network operations – all placed under a government-controlled holding company. By 2017, the holding company will dispose of its shares of savings and insurance companies, which these entities can repurchase. Similar to the case in the privatization of JNOC, the government will possess at least one-third of the shares. In other words, the world's largest bank will be partially controlled by the Japanese government.

Among the issues raised regarding the future of the Postal Accounts Agency as the largest private bank in the world (or, at least, quasi-private) is whether the Japanese mega-banks will remain competitive in domestic and global markets since the bank receives support from the state.[31] In expectation of the privatization, the Postal Bank in 2005 began selling investment trusts, currently offering nine funds that are managed by fund houses with sales predicted to total in 2007 at ¥1,100 billion. It is predicted that the bank will surpass the 50 per cent share that private financial institutions now hold.[32]

Koizumi's legacy: 2004 reform of the State Social Security System at a price

Public opinion polls during the Koizumi years revealed that the electorate would have preferred that Koizumi tackle the Social Security System, which also funds FILP. In 2004, some reforms of the system were enacted but at taxpayers' expense.

The Japanese have developed an abiding mistrust of their Social Security System for a number of reasons:

1. The low fertility rate is causing major concern since 25 per cent of the population is over 65 and the longevity rate is the highest in the world. In 2005, Japan began to lose population and the National Institute for Population and Social Security Research predicts that the proportion of the population aged 65 and older will rise to 27.8 per cent in 2020, while the population of those aged 15 to 64 will fall to 60 per cent. With little immigration and birth-rate that is below replacement (at 1.32), the population of 127 million has already started to shrink.
2. Pension and health-care payouts are swelling as the number of elderly increases.
3. The productive population is shrinking and premium payments are decreasing.

The Social Security System is comprised of pension and health insurance. The Universal (nationwide) Pension System was established in 1961 to cover the self-employed and to include the existing Employees' Pension and various mutual aid pensions. Wage-earners had been insured during the Second World War under the 1944 Employees' Pension Law. The Basic Pension (BP) provides universal coverage and individual benefits are based on the number of years of contribution to the system, regardless of income.

In 1986, the National Pension System was reorganized into two tiers: the BP with fixed benefits and a second tier of remuneration-based benefits to replace the Employees' Pension Insurance (EPI). There were also corporate pension plans that offered more options. Part-time workers are covered by BP, but the state is the insurer.

Public pension costs in 2001 rose to 8 per cent of annual GDP. The 2004 reforms called for tax revenues, equal to one-third of the BP benefits, to be transferred to BP and, in order to cut state spending, to increase patients' share of the costs to 30 per cent because the average stay in hospital in Japan is longer than in other developed countries. It is estimated that by 2025 benefits will be twice that of 2004.[33] The accumulated liabilities or the amount of benefits are said to be approximately ¥570 trillion or 105 per cent of GDP.[34]

The sustainability of this system depends upon how the Japanese view the increases of premiums and the decreases of benefits and how their government's leaders manage the system. The series of scandals involving the National Pension Scheme and the Social Insurance Agency since 2004 that are related here illustrate the deterioration of the system and the difficulties government will experience trying to convince the Japanese to trust the system.

Social Insurance Agency: Special Corporations/IAI

The mutual aid pensions were administrated by three Special Corporations under the administration of national ministries. Due to huge deficits, the three corporations were consolidated in 1997 into one Special Corporation, the Social Insurance Agency. It is one of the world's largest with over 70 million members and $1.3 trillion in reserves.

In 2002, as a part of Koizumi's reform of the public sector, the pension systems of farm, forestry and fishery personnel were consolidated into a single Special Corporation or IAI.

In April 2004 a major scandal erupted when the prime minister, seven cabinet ministers, the leader of the Democratic Party of Japan, and 113 Diet members admitted that they had skipped payment to the National Pension scheme. Prime Minister Fukuda Yasuo, who was the Chief Cabinet Secretary at the time, resigned from Koizumi's Cabinet when it was revealed that he had also withheld payments. Former Prime Minister Koizumi also admitted to missing payments.[35]

The fact that even the highest officials in government had failed to contribute to the National Pension System aggravated the concerns among Japanese that paying into the pension scheme would not necessarily give them full benefits upon retirement simply because there would be fewer young people to contribute.

In May 2007, during Prime Minister Abe Shinzo's administration, the strongest opposition political party, the Democratic Party of Japan (DPJ), revealed that the Social Insurance Agency had lost the records of 50.95 million individuals' payments to the state pension programmes, that 4.3 million records had not been entered into the Social Insurance Agency's computer system and that 280 local governments in charge of collecting the data had destroyed all of the records,[36] triggering an even bigger scandal and Abe's subsequent resignation. The debacle was attributed to massive bureaucratic incompetence. Abe scrambled to restructure the agency, breaking it up into six entities as SIA staff began a mass exodus from the agency. Although 19 retired officials from the Welfare Ministry who were employed in the SIA through *amakudari* returned their summer bonuses to take responsibility, six former officials from the ministry and two former chiefs of the SIA refused. Public outrage escalated when it was revealed in October 2007 that agency employees and local government officials had embezzled ¥400 million from 1966–2006.[37]

Although on 11 July an independent panel was set up to try to assess the credibility of all of the claims, most have not been cleared. The consensus opinion was that it would be difficult to identify 38.5 per cent of the records and that the former heads of the SIA and former welfare ministers were to blame for the mishap. On 14 March 2008, government admitted that the percentage of unidentified public pension accounts that had yet to be matched had risen to 20 million or 40 per cent.[38]

The SIA scandal again emphasized both the motivations of the ministries to establish public corporations in order to provide post-retirement positions for bureaucrats and the ways that Social Security revenue is used to fund public projects. In an interview with the *Japan Times* in July 2007, journalist Iwase Tatsuya, who published two books about the pension problems in 2003 and 2004, claimed that the former Ministry of Health and Welfare had established the pension system in 1961 for the purpose of creating organizations that would provide *amakudari* jobs. He pointed to the Greenpia resorts as one of these organizations that was funded by the Government Pension Investment Fund.

According to the 2006 DPJ Manifesto, the Government Pension Investment Fund diverted pension premiums totalling ¥370 billion to the construction and operation of the resorts, which are located throughout Japan. The resorts were built in the 1980s, but abolished in 2005 due to massive debts.

In 2000, the corporation had amassed a debt of ¥2.3 trillion. The state purchased the land and built the facilities and paid for upkeep, while the Pension Resort Association together with private and public sector companies were the operators. Many bureaucrats became executives in the resorts' operators after their retirement.[39] The government tried to persuade local government to purchase the resorts in order to alleviate taxpayers of the ¥190 billion investment in construction, but to no avail. Government expected to recover only ¥1 trillion through the sale of the resorts, leaving a debt of ¥1.3 trillion.[40]

The manifesto also claimed that pension premiums had been used to purchase golf and massage equipment for SIA officials.

The 2007 DPJ Manifesto pointed to the SIA as an example of how the ministries used Special Corporations for post-retirement positions, contending that 27,882 central government bureaucrats were re-employed in 4576 Special Corporations, independent administrative institutions and other public corporations.

Public funds disbursed to corporations that accept these *amakudari* bureaucrats came to 6 trillion yen in a six-month period. Moreover, improper payouts to the bureaucrats themselves continue with no end in sight. One example is the many past director-generals of the Social Security Agency who cross over to various related public service corporations after they retire, in some cases receiving close to 300 million yen in salary and retirement benefits.

Koizumi's legacy: an increase in public debt

Although Koizumi's reforms centred on the public sector, outstanding government debt had climbed from 140 per cent of annual GDP in 2003 to 180 per cent of annual GDP or ¥546,700 billion at the time of writing. Ultimately, Koizumi was engaged in a tug-of-war with the ministries over territory, in an effort to weaken the bureaucracy and bring more power to the executive office. Despite Koizumi's efforts to dissolve Special Corporations and to cut public funding to all public corporations, the bureaucracy remained in charge of these reforms.

Special Corporations and Independent Administrative Institutions are at the heart of government administration because they perpetuate *amakudari* and the existing civil service system. The interpersonal networks between the ministries and big business encourages bid-rigging for public works projects and, indeed, reports of bid-rigging involving the larger construction companies and the public corporations that distributes contracts for infrastructure works are still common in Japan.

In 1999, J. A. A. Stockwin wrote that *amakudari* is:

> an entrenched institution, driven by structural bureaucratic interests, and also it is a central feature of the way that politics and government work in Japan.[41]

Although it has appeared that Japan has been experiencing social and political changes during the past 15 years as consequences of the bursting of the asset-inflated bubble economy and the ensuing recession, the reality is that the implementation of structural reforms that would serve to promote a stable economic and social system has yet to be realized.

Koizumi's legacy: what fiscal policies perpetuated

Koizumi vowed to cut government spending and he did. But the result is a lopsided economy where contradictions abound. Although trade with China has given Japan's economy a push, only the larger corporations benefit, while small companies continue to languish. Japan's economic malaise has been well documented by both

Japanese and Western media. Bloomberg reported in February 2008 that consumer confidence was at a four-year low. Since wages experienced their biggest fall in three years, retailers are concerned that consumers will prefer to save rather than spend (50 per cent of GDP is generated by consumerism).[42]

Business sentiment among both big and smaller businesses is pessimistic with a 6.3 per cent increase in corporate bankruptcies in 2007 from 2006 (14,091); 99 per cent of the firms were small- and medium-size firms (SMEs). The credit research company Tokyo Shoko Research Ltd. reported on 8 April 2008 that the number of corporate bankruptcies for the fiscal year ending 31 March 2007 was 14,366, with debts that climbed to 6.14 per cent, totalling ¥5.80 trillion. This was the second consecutive year that bankruptcies had increased and the first time in seven years that the remaining debts had increased.[43]

According to a survey conducted by the Shinko Research Institute Co., released on 7 February 2008, over 100 listed companies, including Sony, lowered their predicted earnings for 2007 due to the slowdown in the American economy, the appreciation of the yen and rising oil prices. Since Japan's economy is export-driven, exporters of home electronics and audio-visual equipment were particularly concerned about the economic woes of the United States, which is its largest market.[44]

SME owners are very pessimistic about the future despite the efforts by politicians to access public works contracts and new support programmes (e.g., subsidies and low-interest-rate loans) by METI, the ministry that administrates SME. SMEs, which employ 70 per cent of the workforce, plan to cut capital investment by 10.5 per cent in 2008. Wages at SMEs have fallen 1.9 percent, the fastest rate in 3 and a half years, as smaller companies, burdened with rising costs of materials and oil, were unable to increase winter bonuses.[45] Although a rise in capital investment from large corporations is predicted, in order to trim costs, firms are outsourcing services that previously had been performed in-house by staff under the life-time employment system.

The consequence of cuts in government spending is that regional disparities are widening. In the past many of the prefectures' economies were supported by tax revenue generated by SMEs whose business was dependent primarily upon public works projects.

As businesses continue to fail, Japanese are migrating from rural to urban areas to find work. *Kyodo News* reported on 25 January 2008 that the Internal Affairs and Communications Ministry had released its Basic Resident Register migration statistics, revealing that in 2007, 40 prefectures lost population while only seven prefectures were experiencing a marked increase.[46] Tokyo, the seat of central government, attracted 94,500 migrants from other prefectures because of better job opportunities and Kanagawa received 32,474. Aichi Prefecture, Toyota's headquarters and manufacturing base in Japan, also saw a large inflow of migrants. The largest population outflow was from Hokkaido with 20,267, and Aomori and Nagasaki with 10,272 and 10,064 respectively.

For only the third time in Japan's post-war history, the central government is allowing local governments to issue deficit-covering bonds because of the significant decrease in tax revenue in 2007.[47] The first time was in 1975 when Japan went into recession following the first oil shock, and the second time was in fiscal 2002 after the bursting of the Dot.com bubble in 2001. Eighty local governments who would otherwise experience a deficit will issue bonds totalling ¥180 billion. In previous years, local governments were permitted to release bonds for construction projects only.

Osaka Prefecture, once the financial centre of Japan, is burdened with a ¥5 trillion public debt. As large corporations leave Osaka for Tokyo to gain closer contact with central government, corporate tax revenue has decreased substantially. Experiencing debt for a consecutive nine years, the prefectural government issued ¥200 billion in government bonds in order to continue operating. Governor Hashimoto Toru vowed when he was elected to office on 29 January 2008, that he would reduce the debt by cutting personnel and salaries for prefectural government workers, police officers and teachers.[48] On 6 February, the former lawyer and TV personality met with 500 prefectural workers, telling them that they were effectively working for a bankrupt company.[49] He also had pledged during his campaign to stop the release of government bonds and that the prefecture's budget would not exceed revenue. However, after only one month in office, the new governor was pressured by the prefectural bureaucracy to revise his stance on issuing bonds. In June Hashimoto acknowledged that issuing at least ¥10 billion worth of bonds was necessary to shore up the 2008 fiscal budget.[50]

Government's on-going struggle to trim public spending and government debt is proving to be fruitless. Although on 29 June 2006 former Prime Minister Abe's coalition government pledged to cut spending by ¥11.4 trillion over a five-year period, the Lower House of the National Diet overrode the objections of the Upper House, voting in a ¥1.78 trillion supplementary budget for fiscal 2007. This was the first time since 1993 that a supplementary budget was approved despite the rejection of the Upper House.[51]

On 28 March 2008, despite the rejection by the Upper House, which is controlled by opposition parties, the Diet passed a ¥83 trillion state budget for fiscal 2008. The budget indicates that public debt would inevitably increase, primarily because the LDP is heavily dependent on votes from constituencies in the rural areas which have traditionally relied on public works projects and government subsidies. In the second year of the five-year effort to reduce public debt, public spending will ostensibly be reduced by 3.1 per cent. Since local tax revenue is insufficient, general expenditures will increase by 0.7 per cent in an effort to support regional economies. It had been predicted that regional growth would increase by 16.5 per cent in 2007. Instead, it is a mere 0.2 per cent.[52]

Conservatism according to Abe: Japan Inc. prevails

When Abe Shinzo became prime minister on 26 September 2006, there were high expectations that he would continue to proceed with reforms. But instead of surrounding himself with reformers, he barricaded his office with a clique of old-school LDP conservatives in the image of his grandfather, Kishi Nobusuke, a wartime official in the Ministry of Commerce, Japan's third post-war prime minister and one of the founders of the Liberal Democratic Party.

Abe avoided dealing with reform issues and economic policies, preferring to concentrate on the bills that had been introduced by his predecessors. During his term in office, Abe managed to push through the National Diet a School Education Law the following November that included a provision to instil patriotism in students as well as an amendment that required teachers to renew licences every ten years. The Japan Business Federation (the consolidation of Japan Federation of Economic Organizations and the Japan Federation of Employees Association in 2002) supported these revisions.

However, critics, academics among them, claimed that the bill would give the state control over both public and private educational institutions. Abe also succeeded in upgrading the Defence Agency to a full Ministry of Defence.

The Abe government tried to tackle *amakudari* but met with stiff opposition, not only from the ministries, but also from politicians in both the LDP and the DPJ. The human resource's anti-*amakudari* agency that was established in 2000 arranged re-employment for only one official, despite a $584,700 budget to install a computer system and to publish materials to publicize the agency.[53] Abe abandoned his attempts at civil service reforms only a few months after he tried, but failed to push through the Diet a bill to reform the *amakudari* system. The Internal Affairs and Communications Ministry reported in April 2007 that from 2004 to 2006, approximately 1968 bureaucrats had been assisted by their ministries and agencies to find jobs in companies that had close links to their organizations and that over 500 bureaucrats were from the land ministry, the ministry that administrates the construction industry.

Amakudari for local government officials in both private and public corporations is also common, which promotes bid-rigging for public works contracts at the local level.[54]

During the following year, Abe's administration was dogged by a succession of six scandals involving members of his cabinet, forcing four ministers to resign amidst charges of misappropriation of political funds. The SIA scandal dealt the final blow. After only a year in office, Abe resigned and Japan's economy continued to contract. Deflation remained a key concern among economists.

On 25 September 2007, Fukuda Yasuo assumed the office of Prime Minister. Fukuda, who was 71, is the first prime minister whose father was also a prime minister. An OB in LDP politics and a conservative but one who was considered to be more dovish than Abe, Fukuda focused energies on foreign relations and defence. Like his father Takeo, Fukuda's ties to the ministries were strong.

Abe's book *Toward a Beautiful Country* was published in 2006, shortly before he assumed the post of prime minister. It was a best seller. Abe promoted his ultra- conservative ideology and his intent to perpetuate a national pride through the reconsideration of the chronicling of events of Japan's engagement in Asia during the Second World War, post-war period and the revision of the pacifist constitution in order to allow Japanese military participation in peacekeeping operations abroad. In his book, Abe contended that the term 'conservatism' was regarded negatively and the term 'liberalism' was considered positively. He took refuge in the fact that in recent years, the number of conservative journalists and commentators who espouse nationalism was on the increase.

Abe contended that the Japanese have been a conservative nation for several thousand years and that their society is a conservative system. Abe is correct. In *Special Corporations and the Bureaucracy*, the author quoted a section of a speech that an elite civil servant gave to an audience at Georgetown University Law Center on 7 April 1994, after he was dismissed from the Ministry of International Trade and Industry in December 1993 for creating a job for a former vice-minister's son in MITI, thus enhancing his chances of winning a seat in the National Diet. Naito Masahisa was only the second high-ranking official to be dismissed from MITI since 1952 and the scandal sent shock waves through the ministry. The bursting of the bubble, political turmoil, together with the Naito incident and other scandals in the early 1990s involving elite officials from the Ministry of Finance (MOF) and the Ministry of Construction, sparked public recognition that their system of government administration of the economy was ingrown and corrupt, and that there was a dire need for structural reform of the public sector. But the Japanese cannot reform because of the organic reticence of bureaucrats, businessmen and politicians to initiate changes that would fundamentally change the structure of their system.

Naito had been targeted to become the next Vice-Minister of MITI, the highest post in the ministry, before his dismissal, which was the unfortunate result of a long-standing feud with a former MITI colleague, Kumagai Hiroshi, who, as the Minister of Commerce, Trade and Industry in the Hosokawa Cabinet, had demanded his resignation. After leaving MITI, Naito moved to Georgetown University in Washington, DC, to take a professorship as a participant in the Asia Policy Studies programme. The chair was funded by Marks & Murase, an American law firm that did significant business with Japanese firms and acted as a consultant to the ministries.

In his speech, Naito reflected on the motivations of ministry officials who worked during Japan's rapid economic growth period and who seemed inspired by their roles as the administrators of Japan's economic rebirth. He lamented about the change in attitudes of today's bureaucrats, who, he felt, had become inward and 'turf-conscious', working to protect their ministries' territory rather than making policy to deregulate markets.

Naito told the audience that the Japanese people, who had relied for centuries on either an emperor or a military regime to govern them, did not want to take the initiative to plan their own destiny, but preferred to entrust the responsibility to a bureaucracy. He explained that the submission to bureaucratic rule gave the ministries much power, which was further enhanced by the close contact between bureaucrats and businessmen, who feared retribution if they did not comply with guidance.

Naito did not include the fact that the ministries had extended power over the political economy through their public corporations and the *amakudari* system, and indeed, Naito himself was a part of this system, as is the case for the majority of elite civil servants. Naito was reinstated to MITI in June 2004 as a consultant.

The Japanese view their elite bureaucrats and politicians as separate from themselves. In general, most voters tend to vote for personalities rather than for issues. In the early 1990s, there was a concerted movement by politicians during the Hosokawa and Murayama administration towards political reforms that could have slowed down the further deterioration of Japan's economy, but the momentum for change stopped when the LDP came back to dominate the DIET in 1996.

Ultra-conservatism, along with the system of administration, plays on with the election of Prime Minister Fukuda. The elements explicit to this system are:

1. A rigid hierarchical socio-political system with a bureaucracy invested with the powers to plan and implement Japan's post-war economic growth without being subject to legal sanctions.
2. The close cooperation between business, the bureaucracy and the National Diet that began in the late nineteenth century during the Meiji Restoration. The finely tuned relationship continued before and after the Second World War. Known as the 'iron triangle', it is one of the dominant features in the governing system.
3. A conservative political party that has supported the bureaucracy's policies consistently during Japan's post-war period.

4. The network of former bureaucrats and present bureaucrats throughout business and government that is perpetuated by the *amakudari* system, which greatly enhances bureaucratic power to enforce policy at both the national and local government levels.
5. Significant social pressure to accept bureaucratic policies and guidance.

Accessing the real story: research methodology

The efforts of academics and commentators to access reliable information is complicated by the insularity of organizations and their reticence to open their doors to outside observation by both Japanese and non-Japanese. The Japanese social political system is relatively opaque compared to Western industrialized nations and gaining a solid understanding of a given environment can be difficult and time-consuming. This is particularly true of ministerial operations, because the ministries are very protective of their territory and control the flow of information tightly.

Foreign observers are confronted by the language barrier. Both private and public corporations prefer to use special representatives, who are fluent in English, to communicate with researchers. Many of them have been sent to universities abroad not only to study but, more importantly, to learn how to interact with foreigners so that they can develop the skills to protect and promote their organizations' interests, and to fend off criticism. Japanese observers who are not participants in the organizations they wish to observe will also be accommodated by these representatives.

Japanese and foreign journalists experience difficulties accessing primary data. All journalists covering government activities are assigned to press clubs (*Kisha clubs*) which are offices that are set up to gather news from major organizations such as the ministries, the prime minister's office, political party headquarters, local parliament and police headquarters, as well as consumer, entertainment and sports organizations. Each reporter and journalist from domestic and foreign media is assigned to one club. Accessing a story distributed by other press clubs where they are non-members is problematic and since there are no records of court cases, debates or hearings, they also have difficulties accessing reliable data regarding bureaucratic policies.

The Japan Broadcasting Company (NHK), Nippon Telephone and Telegraph (NTT[55]), Special Corporations/IAIs administered by the Ministry of Public Management, Home Affairs, Posts and Telecommunications, along with Japan Railroad (JR) operate their own press clubs. NHK, like the BBC, is government funded and all viewers are required to pay an annual fee.

There are approximately 1000 press clubs throughout Japan. The membership in each club is approximately 15–20, with the major Japanese dailies regarded as regular club members, although the Diet Club can have as many as 5000 members.

In a Japan Policy Research Institute (JPRI) Working Paper, Laura Freeman discussed the competition for accessing information. The Japan Newspaper Editors and Publishers Association (JNEPA) and the Japan Magazine Publishers Association (JMPA) has access to these clubs but it is common for newspapers and magazines, including the foreign press, to pay members of clubs where they do not have access to leak data or to write stories for publication. Freeman stated:

> The journalists gain a source of extra income and an outlet for some of the information they have obtained but cannot write due to club embargoes and other tacit agreements with members of the club or sources.

Freeman concluded that, although this arrangement benefits both the procurer and the supplier, the public suffers the consequences:

> Under this arrangement, because the magazine has gotten such information second or third hand, it either gets written as a rumor, or because it is written anonymously and/or does not include an attribution of sources (a practice followed by club members and non-members alike), its news value and believability are seriously diminished.[56]

The European Commission in Japan in October 2002 issued *Priority Proposals for Regulatory Reform in Japan*, which called the press clubs 'serious barriers to the free trade of information'. The report stated:

> With the exception of a limited number of wire services (which, if they are members at all, often have only associate membership

and therefore can listen but have no right to ask questions), membership is denied to journalists from foreign media organizations. It is worth noting that shukan-shi, or mass-circulation weekly magazines as well as other weekly, monthly or bi-monthly magazines are also excluded, as well as specialized press covering sectors other than those directly related to the host body.

The report delineated the root of the problem of accessing reliable data, which is cited here:

1. Officials and the hierarchy of the *kisha* club have the means to prevent the spread of information they may consider disadvantageous, on pain of exclusion of the offending journalist from the club. The system thus acts against the public interest, since it may deny or delay access to important information, including, for example, information of direct relevance to public health and safety. Reporting the case of BSE in point.
2. By giving both officials and journalists a vested interest in maintaining the exclusivity of a story, the system encourages over-reliance on a single source of information and a lack of cross-checking, thus diminishing the quality of information available to the wider public.
3. The system encourages the widespread and undesirable practice of split briefings for domestic and foreign journalists, increasing the potential for information to be tailored to one or the other audience by the briefing party, and exacerbating the risk of spreading inaccurate and biased information about Japan.

The commission threatened to raise the problem with the WTO. Although the JNEPA refuted the statement, made in its reply to the accusations, Etienne Reuter, a representative of the commission stated at a December 2003 news conference:

We reject the statement that our proposals are based on misunderstanding, cultural biases and misconception of facts.

The JNEPA acquiesced to the pressure in February 2004 and agreed to allow foreign journalists easier access to government information. Nevertheless, according to Adam Gamble in his book *A Public Betrayed*

(2004), the 2004 reforms are superficial at best. He interviewed journalist Tatsuya Iwase, who condemned the press club system:

> But the Japanese Press Clubs are nothing more than transfer devices. They function and will continue to function as mouthpieces for those interests that hold power in the country because all they [press club journalists] do is a route transfer of the information they are provided by news sources. This is assured, because that is the way they are able to remain close to the power they work with...[57]

Bill Whittaker, who was chief correspondent for CBS Television News from 1989 to 1993, agreed with Freeman's assessment when he was interviewed by the author in 1994 regarding the difficulties in accessing information from Japanese government agencies:

> I do think that the bureaucracy controls the information, not that they manipulate the story but what they choose to reveal and when they choose to reveal it. They play it close to the vest. If they do not want it to get out, it pretty well won't get out. I think that if the bureaucracy decides that the information stays within the bureaucracy, my god, that's where it stays! What I found, also, when it came to the bureaucracy, for the press clubs that operated in different bureaux, if the Secretary [of the particular bureau] said, 'No, you're not going to get that information', that was about the end of it. From what I understood, if a journalist fell into disfavour within his club and its Secretary, he would get even less information the next go-around.[58]

On the other hand, Japanese reporters posted in the United States have expressed that it can be a struggle accessing information from organizations they claim are closed to foreign journalists, particularly in the financial industry. Morinaga Koki was the NHK chief financial correspondent in New York in 1994 when the author interviewed him about his perspectives of the United States and accessing information. He spoke about the barriers that foreign journalists may encounter:

> There are two big forces on Wall Street. One is Jewish. The other is WASP. I struggle to enter their circle. I can catch some

information but it is extremely difficult to enter this silent circle. They are closed. Sometimes I am able to get an interview but in order to get good information I must have a friend among them. I must be a friend to some of them. This is my burden of my assignment here. There are people who control not only the economy but also the politics in the United States. When American journalists cover America they have the advantage. Japanese journalists have the advantage in Japan because perhaps we have many friends in Japan. It is natural that both countries have some barriers. We must get rid of these barriers but it's not a good idea to jump to a conclusion about which country is a more closed society.[59]

It should be noted that NHK correspondents posted abroad will collect data for Japanese government agencies.

Unreliable statistics of macro- and micro-economic data due to the methods of collection and analysis by the ministries can also frustrate research. Eight ministries conduct 55 surveys and statistical research, but the data does not include the service industries and changes in current economic conditions. The Internal Affairs and Communication Ministry submitted a bill in January 2007 that would revise the statistics law that was enacted 60 years ago in 1947.[60] However, there have been a number of efforts since the late 1990s to reform the methods of gathering official data. The research by Japanese scholars is often funded through public corporations administered by the national ministries and the research regarding such subjects as Special Corporations has been considered to be politically indiscrete.

Bill Whittaker succinctly pointed to a fundamental reason why Western commentators have misinterpreted the characteristics of Japan's model of administration:

I think what fools you, what is seductive but on the surface is that it looks familiar. You've got tall buildings, freeways, subways and Western dress and all sorts of things that can lull you into feeling that you can relate to it and understand ... But if you're there for a while, you begin to realize that it is just a thin veneer, that the real Japan is behind or beneath that thought, that Western thought.

The author chose work in specific organizations that afforded the opportunity to experience as fully as possible Japan's corporate environment, government administration of the private and public sectors and Japan's media coverage of foreign affairs, in order to access information that would promote a more realistic, and also a more objective assessment of the Japanese system. The effort to achieve objectivity requires integration into these sectors. The research culminated in an analysis that is based principally on the Japanese perspective of their system and their continuing dilemma.

The book's objectives

The following chapters in Part I examine the institutional factors in the Japanese system of government administration that have paralysed the decision-making process and prevented the system from adapting to the ever-changing demands on the domestic front and in the global political economy. There is discussion both of the development of the current system of government administration of the political economy from a historical perspective and the socio-political factors that perpetuate the intimate relationship between bureaucracy, business and politics. Chapters 4 and 5 illustrate the interpersonal networks in the 'ruling triad' through the *amakudari* system, which binds the bureaucracy with business and which enhances bureaucratic control over the implementation of policies at both the national and local levels.

Part II focuses on the ministerial system, including the training of the elite ministry officials and how they cope with their system. Excerpts from interviews the author conducted in 1994 with civil servants from the central ministries and prefecture governments on loan to a Special Corporation in the United States provide rare insights of how bureaucrats regard themselves in the civil service system and how they perceive America, Japan's protector in the Pacific and largest trading partner until China forged ahead as Number One in 2008.

The interviews are extremely relevant to the economic dilemma that the Japanese are facing currently due to Japan's dependency on the United States. The interviews reveal a significant degree of defensiveness regarding Japan's relationship not only with the United States, but also Japan's position in the global political economy in general. Although 15 years have passed since the interviews were conducted, the mind-set of Japanese ministerial officials towards the United States remains the same and parallels can be drawn with their approach to other economic powers, namely China, South Korea and Russia, and how economic and foreign policies may be planned in the future.

In a deeper sense, the interviews provide an invaluable insight into why the Japanese have yet to integrate into the international community.

2
The Development of the System

> Most of the ideas for economic growth came from the
> bureaucracy, and the business community reacted with the
> attitude of what one scholar called 'responsive dependence'.
>
> (Johnson, 1982)[1]

The 'ruling triad'

The Japanese describe their governing system as a 'ruling triad' of
conservative politicians, elite bureaucrats, and leading businessmen
(sei kan zai). These institutions are bound together by elements
inherent in the Japanese socio-political system, resulting in a deep
and abiding relationship.

In Japan 'bureaucracy' and 'bureaucrat' refer to the elite officials
in each agency at the national level who plan and implement policy.
It is generally recognized that the bureaucracy is the government's
most powerful entity.[2]

Prior to the 1990s, it was commonly viewed by both Japanese and
non-Japanese scholars that the policies of the Japanese ministries,
principally the fiscal and industrial policies forged by the Ministry of
Finance (MOF) and the Ministry of International Trade and Industry
(MITI) respectively, propelled Japan's post-war rapid economic growth.
Regardless of these views even before the Arab Oil Embargo in October
1973 (referred to as the 'first Oil Shock'), cracks began to appear in
MITI's industrial policy for developing the energy-intensive industries.

MITI as well as the other ministries were determined in the
continuation of mercantile policies and the protection of domestic

industry from foreign competition, with stiff regulations and recession cartels that promoted collusion and price-fixing among Japanese manufacturers. Nevertheless, scholars continued to extol the skills of an elite class of bureaucrat who appeared to put the state before personal gain. But the image of the skill and the dedication of elite career officials that had been well-documented by both academics and commentators worldwide was tarnished in the early 1990s by a number of scandals regarding collusion between the ministries and business. Consequently, a disillusioned public began to closely scrutinize the civil service system, principally the *amakudari* system and public corporations. Furthermore, with the possibility of *amakudari* positions decreasing in businesses, a career in the national ministries was losing its lustre. Younger bureaucrats were terminating their careers to enter the private sector.

As Masahito Naito explained to his Georgetown University audience, the Japanese rely on their elite civil servants and politicians. Civil servants in the national ministries have remained aloof from the general population, while keeping close contact with businesses through their network of retired officials who migrate from public to private corporations. The ministries struggle to maintain territory, while trying to poach territory from the others' industrial sectors can intensify the relationship with the private sector.

A historical perspective of the development of the system will explain why the Japanese endowed elite bureaucrats with power and prestige.

The Meiji Period (1868–1912): in the beginning

The Japanese regard their system of bureaucratic administration as remaining fundamentally unchanged since its inception in 1887 during the Meiji Restoration and that it is still steeped in semi-feudalism, despite the end of a military ruler (*Shogun*) whose xenophobic policies effectively isolated a feudal Japan from the rest of the world for over 200 years. This period is known as the Tokugawa Era, named for the military leaders who effectively quelled the wars between clans to bring peace and stability to the country. Foreign traders from primarily Spain, Portugal, Holland and Britain had been allowed entry to Japan, but the *Shogun*, fearing that his retainers were being unduly influenced by the interests of some of the traders and that the introduction of Catholicism by Portuguese and Spanish priests would change the values of the Japanese thus jeopardizing the military's control over the population, closed Japan to foreign trade and prohibited the practice of the Christian religion. Limited trade was allowed with the Dutch through Nagasaki, a port in the third largest island of Kyushu.

The Tokugawa government (*bakufu*) controlled 25 per cent of the land and the cities which were important economically. The retainer-administrators of the *Shogun*'s domains were known as *samurai*, some of who served as soldiers to protect the lands from encroachment by clans from other domains. In 1867, a civil war between supporters of the military regime and the chiefs of the western domains led by the Satsuma and Choshu clans brought down the Tokugawa government. The downfall of the *shogunate* is generally credited to the American Admiral Matthew Perry, who entered unannounced with his war ships into Uraga Bay in 1853 to demand, on behalf of the United States, that Japan open its shores to trade with the United States. But prior to Perry's surprise visit, the *Shogun* was already experiencing unrest among the Japanese, who had become discontented with economic policies. The policies focused on controlling and regulating an agricultural economy, increasing productivity of the land to provide the government with as much tax revenue as possible. By 1800, farmers were not permitted to engage in any work other than producing food and if they did not meet a quota, they could be punished for non-compliance (disobedience). It can be argued that these policies of regulation of production paralleled some of the policies employed by the post-war economic ministries, who did not rely on market mechanisms to drive Japan's post-war industrial development.

The subsequent signing of trade treaties with the Western powers (America, Britain and Holland)[3] gave foreigners the right to reside in the port cities set down in the treaties and removed Japan's claim to set its own tariffs. The Japanese trade negotiators were the future leaders of the new Meiji government.[4]

From 1854–65, the *shogun* and his retainers in the western domains tried unsuccessfully to build a defence system against encroachment from the west. During this time, two of the western clans, the Satsuma and Choshu, gained a power base which resulted in a political struggle with the *shogun* and his other retainers, who were concerned about the growing strength of the two clans. The failure to reach a compromise regarding the establishment of a government that could create an economically and militarily strong nation able to defend itself against occupation by foreign powers triggered the revolt against the *shogun,* bringing over 200 years of isolationism to an end.

In 1868, a constitutional monarchy was established by members of the Satsuma and Choshu clans and aristocrats. In 1871, a government was consolidated, feudal domains were abolished, prefectures were established under central government control, and the Ministry of Education was established. Okubo Toshimichi, a *samurai* from the Satsuma clan who was instrumental in the overthrow of the *shogun,* was one of the key planners of the Meiji government. He understood the importance of forging economic policies that would bring Japan on to the same industrial and economic plateau as America and Europe. Okubo and members of the new government travelled extensively around America and Europe from 1871–73 in the first diplomatic mission, known as the Iwakura Mission (led by Prince Iwakura Tomomi), to collect information about educational systems, technologies, economic and political systems that would assist in Japan's industrialization. The delegation also tried to renegotiate the trade agreements, which were considered to favour America and Britain.

The consensus was that government-led industrialization would culminate in private initiative as the private sector matured. John Sagers stated:

> From Okubo's perspective, economic prosperity was intimately tied to national power. The Meiji government's goal was to enrich the Japanese people by helping them as much as possible. The state was committed to the people's prosperity in enterprise, but within the context of serving the national interest as defined by government bureaucrats, not foreign economic theories.[5]

Sager contended that Okubo's policies for Japan's rapid economic development emanated from his visit in 1872 to Britain where he studied England's economic development, which had been based on mercantile policies and the protection of domestic markets through laws that gave only British ships the right to bring imports into British ports. Okubo concluded that government intervention in the process of industrialization and mercantile policies would spur Japan's economic growth.

The government would have to work closely with the Japanese private sector to solve real world problems.[6]

Okubo served as Finance Minister in 1871, initiating the Land Tax Reform. He was also the Minister of Home Affairs and he used the ministry to promote industrialization. He abolished some of the entitlements of the *samurai*, such as the right to wear swords in public and to receive wages which came from the rice tax revenues in silver, the currency at the time. Instead, one-third of the wages was paid out in government bonds.

Okubo never saw his industrial policies come to fruition. When members of the Satsuma clan who were discontented with Okubo's policies rebelled in 1877 against the government's new army, which was established and led by Okubo as the Home Minister, and were defeated, many of the Satsuma clan regarded Okubo as a traitor. In May 1878, he was assassinated by members of his own clan.

The Ministry of Public Works was established to aid in industrial development and to produce the same products domestically that were being imported. However, by the late 1870s Japan's trade deficit had spiralled and government spending escalated. Import substitution policies were terminated and production for export, such as silk yarn and tea, was promoted by the Ministry of Home Affairs in cooperation with local governments. By the 1880s, the policies that promoted government-led industrial development had been undermined when many of the state-owned companies experienced a deficit and were subsequently sold to private enterprises.

In 1881, the Ministry of Agriculture and Commerce (MAC) was established to institute agrarian reforms, to promote new farming technologies brought from the West and to guide industrialization. The Bank of Japan (BOJ), Japan's central bank, was established the following year and was at the foundation of Japan's industrialization. Due to the funding of the new military and the suppression of the Satsuma Rebellion, government debt soared. The resulting inflation induced the government to consolidate the banking system.

The 135 government authorized national banks that had been established were given the right to print bank notes. In 1877, due to inflation, the government limited the amount of yen notes printed by each bank. After the BOJ was established, it monopolized the right to issue bank notes. The gold standard was adopted in 1897 (most of the industrialized European countries had adopted the gold standard by 1880).

In 1885, the first Cabinet system was established. A constitution modelled on Bismarck's Prussian constitution was passed into law in 1889 and a bicameral Parliament was inaugurated in 1890. The first general elections were held the same year, culminating in the opening of the First Diet (Japan's Parliament).

But the pre-Meiji military mind-set remained fundamentally unchanged. Yamagata Aritomo is considered to be the major architect of the Meiji bureaucracy. He was a Choshu *samurai* who participated in the overthrow of the *Shogun* in 1867–68 as a staff officer. One of seven political leaders known as *genro*, Yamagata played a number of key roles in Japan's initial military and political development. As the War Minister in the first Cabinet he laid the foundation for the Imperial Japanese Army. And as the Home Minister (1883–87), he worked tirelessly to suppress political parties as well as labour movements. He was the third prime minister (24 December 1889 to 6 May 1891) and also served a second term of office (8 November 1898 to 19 October 1900).

The persona of the elite bureaucracy was enhanced by Yamagata when in 1889, he pushed through the Civil Service Appointment Ordinance regarding the behaviour of civil servants that effectively kept political parties from intervening in the bureaucracy. Yamagata's amendment advanced the power of an elite bureaucracy, which he guaranteed until his death in 1922. Yamagata's tenacity led to an autocratic governing system with the bureaucracy dominating the political process. Since that time, policy-making has been consistently guided by elite officials and the legislation written by the elite bureaucracy has been consistently supported by elected officials in the National Diet.

Retired elites run for political office and have served as members of cabinets and prime ministers. Many of the present ranking elite bureaucrats' and elected officials' ancestors were of the samurai class. Abe Shinzo himself descends from the Choshu clan, which was duly noted when he assumed the office of prime minister. Abe's roots are in Yamaguchi Prefecture, located in Choshu. Abe's father was a career politician in the LDP whose constituency was in Shimonoseki, a large port city in Yamaguchi. Upon his death in 1991, Abe inherited the full support of his father's constituency, giving him a large majority in the election. Prime Minister Abe's objectives were said to resemble his Choshu forefathers' policies which prioritized the national interest.

The first Meiji Cabinet began the task of educating the new breed of civil servants by opening Tokyo Imperial University (now known as Tokyo University or *Todai*) in1887 and designing a special civil service entrance exam for the ministries. Since that time, graduates from the law faculty in Tokyo University have had the best opportunities for gaining entry into the elite classes of the ministries and for promotion to the top echelons in the ministries.

Japan's government made an all-out effort to achieve economic and industrial equality with the Western powers that had pressured Japan to enter into trade agreements in 1853. The Meiji government was determined not to allow occupation by foreign powers. The slogan at the time was 'Prosperous Country, Strong Country, Strong Military'. The government imported technologies from the West, employing over 3000 European and American railroad and marine engineers, financial and legal consultants, military instructors, agricultural experts and educators to train the Japanese. Simultaneously, the government sent Japanese abroad to study Western methods of production, including that of iron, shipbuilding, and paper as well as the education, military, medical, engineering and legal systems.

Ministerial cooperation with family-owned oligopolies (*zaibatsu*)

Guy DeJonquieres wrote in the 14 June 2005 issue of the *Financial Times*:

> In much of East Asia, market domination by powerful incumbents has kept domestic competition weak and entry barriers high above all in the stunted and overprotected service sector. Incestuous ties between governments and producers perpetuate archaic and capricious regulatory systems that serve to preserve the established

order, not to promote the flexible markets, innovation and sound commercial practices.

The article's title is 'East Asia's model needs an overhaul'. The East Asian model is based on Japan's post-war model of government administration of rapid economic growth, which resembles Japan's government administration of industry during the Second World War system.

Countries that industrialized prior to the twentieth century are commonly referred to as market economies or social market economies, where government controls over economic and social policies are not as intense as compared to countries that have developed industrially during the twentieth century, where government intervention is intrinsic to the system of administration.

Countries that are currently developing industrially are known as 'developmental states', a term coined by such political economy scholars as Chalmers Johnson[7] to explain the phenomenon of state-led macroeconomic planning in East Asia. The term was first used to describe Japan's post-war industrial development which was guided by MITI, through an industrial policy that was mercantile and protectionist. It was thought in the 1980s that Japan would develop into a market economy as the government would gradually deregulate markets and open Japan to foreign competition. But as was previously stated, FDI in Japan is the lowest of all of the industrialized countries and is testimony to the fact that, although Japan is fully industrialized, the ministries are unwilling to relinquish their territories.

The so-called 'incestuous ties between governments and producers' can be traced to the late nineteenth century. The construction of infrastructure such as railway lines was vital for the allocation of raw materials and the distribution of goods. Since government funds were constrained and borrowing from foreign banks was limited, the private sector stepped in with large capital investment. This was the case in most large-scale industries, including the development of heavy industries and shipbuilding during the early twentieth century.

Large family-owned oligopolies cooperated closely with the government to propel Japan's rapid industrialization. The oligopolies, known as *zaibatsu* (wealthy cliques), were large conglomerates whose controlling interests were dominated by a single family and who engaged in merchant banking, trade, mining and manufacturing. Mitsui originally engaged in money changing and kimono shops on appointment to the *shogunate* during the eighteenth century. Mitsubishi began operations during the Meiji Period (1870) with a contract from the government to operate steamships.

The Ministry of Agriculture and Commerce (MAC) was instrumental in guiding industrial development, managing and regulating the production of machinery, shipbuilding and heavy industries. The musket and cannon arsenals built by the feudal lords during the Tokugawa Era were banned, and arsenal workers were transferred to government-operated mills and retrained by foreign engineers in machinery production and shipbuilding. The mass production of steel commenced at the Osaka Armoury in 1890 after the installation of Japan's first open-hearth furnace. At the time, Japan was producing only 1000 tons of steel, relying on 90,000 tons of imported steel to fill the demand. The government established the steel producer Yawata to accelerate production and the *zaibatsu* followed government's lead. The Sumitomo Steel, Kawasaki Steel, Kobe Steel, and the Nippon Steel Pipe Companies were all operating by 1912. By 1914, through the use of the open-hearth furnace, the new steel companies succeeded in producing 44 per cent of rolled steel and 64 per cent of pig iron for domestic use.

Cotton Yarn was an early important mainstay of industry with heavy investment from wealthy merchants. By 1907 Japan was a major exporter of cotton yarn, as large companies formed oligopolies, driving British yarn from the domestic market.

The Industrial Bank of Japan (IBJ) was established in 1900 as a key support mechanism for industrial development to introduce foreign capital. However, government limited foreign direct investment to protect immature industries.

Japan's victory against China in the Sino-Japanese War, 1894–95, revealed the surprising strength of Japan's fledging military. A territorial dispute over Korea continued, with a subsequent war with Russia (1904–05). Again, to Russia's surprise, Japan was victorious, gaining Korea as a ceded territory from 1910 until the end of the Second World War. Through its victories against China and Russia, Japan began its initial expansion into southern Manchuria. As Japan expanded into East Asia, Japanese companies began investing in the development of resources and infrastructure in these territories.

Taisho period: the age of liberalism

The Emperor Meiji died in 1912. During his successor Emperor Taisho's reign (1912–26) great advances were seen in the smoke-stack industries as the cooperation between the oligopolies and the ministries continued.

Japan's economic growth benefited substantially during the First World War through the export of military supplies, ships, coal and steel to the Allied Powers. Imports of textiles, chemicals and machinery ceased and the Japanese had to expand production to meet domestic demand. Although imports to Japan decreased, exports of military supplies, cargo ships, coal and steel to the United States, Great Britain and France flourished. From 1913–19, total manufacturing output rose approximately 150 per cent. Prior to the war, Japan was a debtor nation that imported goods and services from America and Europe. But as the export-led economic boom continued, it became a creditor nation with a trade surplus.

Although the Japanese saw no action during the war, Japan took advantage of Germany's engagement in Europe, which weakened its military position in the port cities it leased from China. Japan declared war on Germany in 1914, and swiftly occupied Shandong Province as well as the Mariana, Caroline and Marshall Islands in the Pacific. Japan also declared war on China, presenting the Twenty-One Demands on 15 January 1915. The Twenty-One Demands was a document in the form of two treaties which ostensibly ensured peace in Asia, but gave Japan the leverage to expand into Manchuria and Inner Mongolia and request joint ownership of large mining and metallurgical facilities in central China. Japanese companies began to invest capital in the construction of railway lines and the operation of the coal and silver mines with the support of the ministries and the military.[8]

By 1919, Japan had successfully entered the global political arena. And as testimony to this, Japan was included among the five powers represented at the Versailles Peace Conference and was granted a permanent seat on the Council of the League of Nations (forerunner of the United Nations). The peace treaty corroborated Japan's rights in Shandong Province, which enraged the Chinese who waged anti-Japanese protests. The Pacific islands were also mandated to Japan.

But the end of the war in 1918 marked the beginning of economic and political turmoil and a series of recessions and financial crises that prompted the beginning of the Second World War system. The shipbuilding industry saw a marked decline in orders, a surplus of war ships and depressed prices. As orders declined, Japan slipped in the ranks to ninth among shipbuilding nations. The oligopolies countered by diversifying production into automobiles, aircraft and general machinery.[9]

Although by 1919, Japan's economy was booming because of post-war construction activities, expanded exports and new business start-ups, a stockmarket crash on 15 March 1920 triggered a panic. Stockrooms overflowed with inventories of raw silk, cotton textiles and rice as businesses went bankrupt. The government and the BOJ reacted as lender of last resort, supplying substantial funds to banks for providing loans to key industries and to prop up the stockmarket.

Regardless of the banking crisis, the heavy and chemical industries were developed through a number of joint ventures between Japanese firms and Japanese and American firms. Mitsubishi Corporation was a major player, operating through subsidiaries in Germany and France to import technologies and patents. Mitsubishi Shipbuilding and Mitsubishi Heavy Industries shared about 30 patent rights and manufacturing licenses. Mitsubishi Electric signed a cooperation contract with Westinghouse to share technologies.

By the 1920s, the *zaibatsu* had established holding companies that monitored and audited their affiliated firms. The companies also issued joint shares of stocks. New *zaibatsu* were formed as well. As an example, Nissan was established in 1928 to replace Kuhara, a *zaibatsu* that had unsuccessfully engaged in commodity speculation.[10]

The Taisho period is sometimes referred to as the 'Taisho Democracy' or the 'age of liberalism' because it marked a brief respite from the traditional governing system and a transition to a parliamentary democracy, as illustrated by Prime Minister Takashi Hara who assumed office in September 1918. He recognized that the key political issue confronting the Japanese was the tension between politicians and bureaucrats (non-elected officials). Hara boldly sought to weaken the bureaucracy by firing bureaucrats in local government and other public employees, and replacing them with people, regardless of background and rank, whom he regarded as talented and who would contribute to planning long-term economic policies for both national and regional development. His opponents were the military and officials from Kagoshima and Yamaguchi (formerly Satsuma and Choshu).

However, from 1923 onward a series of events precipitated the end of the age of liberalism. The economy was dealt yet another blow when the Great Kanto Earthquake hit the Tokyo-Yokohama region in 1923. The government borrowed heavily from the BOJ and implemented a ¥400 million disaster relief bill. Due to the imports of massive quantities of goods for reconstruction, Japan's trade surplus disappeared while its trade deficit escalated.

The Japanese were becoming more discontented with government policy as government debt increased. There was a call for universal suffrage, allowing everyone to vote regardless of income. Students along with professors and journalists, supported by labour unions, socialists, communists and anarchists, launched large but peaceful demonstrations. Hara allowed the protests, which proved to be fatal. He was assassinated in 1921 at Tokyo Station by a railroad worker who was a right-wing sympathizer. From 1922 to the end of the Second World War in 1945, Japan was served by 22 Prime Ministers and 11 were either retired generals or admirals, with the exception of Tojo Hideki, who was an acting general.

Corporate diversification into the heavy industries initiated certain systems that continued during Japan's post-war economic development. The large producers set up their private training facilities to train skilled labour and to ensure that its workers did not migrate to other businesses or join labour unions. The seniority system (promotion and wages according to the length of employment in firms) also originated during this time. By the 1920s, labour unions had been formed to represent workers and farmers.

Additionally, the post-war *keiretsu* system can be traced to this time. The smaller firms did not have the capital to finance the training of skilled labour and had to rely predominantly on unskilled labour. Unable to compete with the larger companies, they began to operate as suppliers of manufactured components and other goods and services.

The Showa period and the empowerment of bureaucracy: an enduring relationship with the oligopolies and the development of industrial policy

Emperor Showa assumed the throne upon the death of Emperor Taisho in 1926. His reign continued until 1989, the longest for a Japanese ruler. The present government administration of Japan's socio-economy began during the early Showa Period.

At the end of 1926, the government was able to reimburse the BOJ only half of the loans and a banking crisis ensued. On 18 April 1927, the Japanese branch of the Bank of Taiwan suspended operations, followed by five more banks on 21 April. The *zaibatsu* took full advantage of the crisis and gained controlling interests in the banks, and took over smaller companies through purchasing equities and placing their executives on the firms' boards. Although the financial crisis directly affected only the banking sector, the economy continued in a series of recessions.

The recession and the economic slowdown brought more power to the bureaucracy. In 1925, to deal with the mounting economic problems, the Ministry of Agriculture and Commerce (MAC) split into two ministries, the Ministry of Agriculture and the Ministry of Commerce and Industry (MCI). MCI authorized recession cartels[11] that covered the majority of industries. It subsidized businesses to promote exports in order to counteract the trade deficit. The recession cartels, the subsidization of business, and industrial rationalization formed the foundation of MCI's industrial policy, a term used to describe government guidance of economic and industrial development at the macro- and microeconomic levels. All governments plan industrial policies, which are forged to help support industries that are considered vital to national interests, through a set of policy instruments that may include the regulation of production, tax incentives to domestic companies that procure from domestic suppliers, subsidization of R&D, long-term, low-interest rate loans to businesses for expansion, and protection of industry from foreign competition from imports through tariff taxes.

1927 marked a fundamental strengthening of the alliance between the bureaucracy and big business. The Commerce and Industry

Deliberation Council, an organization whose members were from private industry, was established in 1927, and continued until 30 July 1930.[12] The organization was the predecessor of the current Industrial Structure Council. With the cooperation of the Council, MCI planned policy to protect industry from the depression. It is at this time that the concept of industrial rationalization developed. MCI established the Industrial Rationalization Deliberation Council on 19 November 1929.

In *MITI and the Japanese Miracle: The Growth of Industrial Policy*, Chalmers Johnson chronicled the advent of industrial rationalization and industrial policy. He defined industrial rationalization thus:

> industrial rationalization means state policy at the micro-level, state intrusion into the detailed operations of individual enterprises with measures intended to improve those operations (or, on occasion, to abolish the enterprise).[13]

Yoshino Shinji, who was the head of MCI's Industrial Affairs Bureau, formed the Temporary Industrial Rationalization Bureau (TIRB) on 2 June 1930 to operate semi-autonomously of MCI. The TIRB planned policies for the control of businesses, set industrial standards and provided subsidies to support consumer consumption and the production of goods.[14] Yoshino became Vice-Minister of the ministry in 1931. One of his protégés was Kishi Nobusuke, an assistant section chief in the Secretariat, whom he sent to Germany in 1931 to investigate German industrial rationalization policies.

Upon graduating from Tokyo Imperial University, Kishi entered MCI in 1920. In 1935, he became one of the top officials and a key planner in the industrial development of Manchuko in Manchuria. Prime Minister, General Tojo Hideki, prime minister from 1941 until Japan's defeat in 1945, who was in charge of military operations in Manchuria, supported Kishi in Manchuko. During his administration in 1941 he appointed Kishi as Cabinet Minister of Commerce and Industry.

MCI expanded its control over industry through the Important Industries Control Law, which was drafted by members of the TIRB and passed by the Diet on 25 February 1931. The law gave the ministry the right to form cartels in 26 industries, such as rayon, paper, cotton spinning, shipbuilding, electrical machinery, iron and steel, considered vital to national interests.[15] Sugar manufacturing, beer brewing, carbide manufacturing and flour milling also were deemed important industries. Significantly, the law also laid the foundations for the use of the 'administrative guidance' policy tool, which has been used consistently by MITI to issue directives to industries to form cartels, to fix prices and to regulate production during Japan's post-war development.

The Great Depression triggered by the Wall Street Stockmarket Crash in 1929 profoundly affected Japan's economy and threw the country into political turmoil, the prelude to militarism and the war with China. Prime Minister Tanaka Giichi, Japan's prime minister from 1927–29, sent troops to China to obstruct Chiang Kai-shek's Kuomintang Party's efforts to unify the country. Although the action was unauthorized by government, Japanese troops from Guangdong Province set about protecting Japanese interests in Manchuria in June 1928.

When he assumed office in 1931, Japan's twenty-ninth prime minister, Inukai Takayuki, attempted to cut government expenditure by reining in an expanding military budget. However, the Manchurian Incident in 1931 brought about Inukai's assassination by army officers in 1932. The Manchurian Incident was the bombing of a railway station under construction by the Japanese in Mukden in southern Manchuria. Fearing that Japan's interests would be threatened by the Kuomintang, the army, despite the protests of politicians, used the incident as an excuse to set up a puppet state in Manchuria in 1932.

Again the military action in Mukden was unauthorized and, although only some of the officers who were involved in Inukai's assassination were tried and sentenced to prison terms, they were also regarded as patriots. The army continued its forays into Shanghai, engaging with the Chinese ostensibly to protect Japanese interests in Manchuria. Although the government was formally opposed to the military action, the army received popular support.

On 26 February 1936, 1400 junior army officers attempted a *coup d'état* by seizing key government buildings in Tokyo and assassinating three high-ranking officials. However, they were foiled in their attempt to assassinate the prime minister. Although many of the rebels were imprisoned, only a small number of the officers were executed.

Second World War: the intensification of ministerial powers

The military budget was increased substantially in 1936, following which Japan declared war on China in July 1937. The advent of the war gave the economic ministries, MCI and the Ministry of Finance (MOF), more control over the industrial and banking sectors, as well as a closer alliance with the oligopolies who produced armaments and military supplies. A close partnership was an inevitable result of the all-out effort to win the war in the Pacific. The major *zaibatsu* operating in 1937 were Mitsui, Mitsubishi, Sumitomo, Furukawa, Nissan, Yasuda, Okura, Nomura and Asano.[16]

Emergency legislation was enacted, which allowed bureaucrats to mobilize the economy. In 1937 the pro-military Cabinet pushed three laws through the Diet that effectively gave the state extensive controls:

1. The Export-Import Commodities Emergency Measure Law, which gave the munitions industry priority for the allocation of vital materials such as raw materials and chemicals.
2. The Emergency Capital Allocation Law was used to give the munitions industry priority treatment, controlling the establishment of firms, dividend payments, capital increases, bond flotation and loans.
3. The Munitions Industrial Mobilization Law extended bureaucratic command over production.

In 1938 the General Mobilization Law was passed, giving the state complete control over society. The three institutions that played the key roles in administrating the wartime economy were MCI, MOF and the BOJ. MCI managed and regulated industry as a whole, as well as munitions production. On 1 November 1943, MCI merged with the Cabinet Planning Board to form the Ministry of Munitions (MM) in order to improve production of military supplies. Although Prime Minister Tojo Hideki, the former Vice-Minister of War, was the MM's first Vice-Minister, his deputy Kishi Nobusuke oversaw operations.

The BOJ poured funds into both the banks that were established by MCI and MOF and to private banks (the large ones were *zaibatsu* banks) to finance the production of goods considered vital for military supplies, particularly munitions. The Industrial Bank of Japan (IBJ), administered by MCI and MOF, was a crucial support mechanism, providing funds for munitions. Motor companies such as Toyota, Nissan and Isuzu produced trucks for the military. The IBJ remained an important financer of industry during Japan's post-war economic growth until 2001, when it was merged with two private metropolitan banks.[17]

In 1944, the 'System of Financial Institution Authorized to Finance Munitions Companies' was established, the bill giving the government the authority to order private banks run by the *zaibatsu* to fund munitions manufacturers, thus ensuring a steady supply of armaments. Each bank was assigned to one munitions firm. In 1945, MOF established two banks to allocate funds to over 600 firms, assigned to fulfil their production quotas. The banks were called 'Financial Institutions Authorized to Finance Munitions Companies' and this system continued as the 'main bank' system until the 1990s. The banks were protected against risky lending through government loan guarantees. By 1945, 2000 firms, many of them not engaged in the production of military supplies, had been assigned a bank that would be in charge of their needs. By the end of the war, bank credit accounted for 100 per cent of corporate funding. The post-war formation of the giant financial groups known as *keiretsu* is a consequence of this close relationship between the *zaibatsu* and the main bank system.[18]

Social welfare and corporate culture

The mobilization of the wartime economy brought about some important changes in the corporate culture and human resource management that have remained relatively unchanged throughout Japan's post-war economic development. Trade and industrial unions, which had originated in the 1920s, became more popular during the war as MCI's controls over industry intensified.

In the 1930s, groups of corporations similar to the *zaibatsu* became prevalent, which increased the powers of corporate management because the new shareholders were eager for high growth. Shareholders interests were eliminated, managers were given more power, and employees were motivated through company unions and job security. Trade unions were abolished and substituted with corporate in-house union activities. Companies set up Industrial Patriotic Societies that held joint meetings between management and employees to discuss concerns and management decisions. This effectively eliminated strikes and the disruption of production.

The Employees Pension Insurance Fund for salaried workers was established in 1944. Takeo Hanazawa, a section chief in the former Ministry of Health and Welfare 1942–45, wrote in a book edited by one of his ministry's organizations in 1988 that the establishment of the pension fund gave the bureaucrats a great sense of power:[19]

> We can create foundations such as an employee's pension insurance fund and top officials have power equivalent to the Bank of Japan governor. After welfare ministry officials retire, they would have no difficulty finding jobs.

Although the bureaucracy was endowed with the legal capacity to operate free from political interference during the Meiji Period, it was during the war, through the intense state intervention in the Japanese economy, that the institutional mind-set of management of Japan's post-war economy was established. The extra-legal authority that the bureaucracy enjoys today is connected to the wartime system of government administration and is perpetuated by institutional mechanisms that are discussed in the following chapters.

3
The Elite Bureaucracy:
The Image of Reform

> ...for all intents and purposes Japan's wartime economic controls remained unchanged after World War II. The very bureaucracy and managers, who had demonstrated excellence in running the fully mobilized economy, whether in Manchuria or back home, received rapid promotion in the post-war system.
>
> (Werner, 2003)[1]

The United States' abiding military presence in Japan and its open markets to Japanese exports during Japan's post-war years has played a fundamental role in keeping the Japan system intact and the bureaucracy in the seat of power. By the time Japan had achieved the third highest GDP in the world in 1970 (behind the United States and the Soviet Union respectively), the old-style bureaucracy and an ultra-conservative political system was firmly entrenched.

The period 1945–52 is commonly referred to as the Allied Occupation. The occupying countries were the United States, Great Britain and Australia. Great Britain and Australia sent far fewer troops than the United States, which was commanded by General Douglas MacArthur, the Supreme Commander of the Allied Powers (SCAP). The objectives of the occupation were three-fold: Japan's demilitarization and democratization; the purging of war criminals; and Japan's economic resuscitation. The United States was determined to create a capitalist and democratic society.

SCAP fully intended to reform Japan's wartime economic system by systematically disbanding the military and the ministries (the Munitions Ministry was abolished in 1945, along with the Home Ministry and the military police), dismantling the *zaibatsu*, dissolving the constitutional monarchy, and initiating a new constitution to introduce democratic principles such as freedom of speech, free elections and female suffrage. Labour unions were allowed to organize and the Socialist and Communist Parties that had been banned during the war were also given the right to reorganize.

However, by the end of the Occupation in 1952, SCAP had actually succeeded in endowing the ministries with more power than they had held during the war. The Occupation was scheduled to end by 1948 with a Western-style liberal and democratic governing system in place. A new constitution, which removed the Showa emperor as the formal head of state, replaced the Meiji Constitution in 1947. The famous Article 9 renounced Japan's right to wage war.[2] But the beginning in 1945 of the Cold War with the Soviet Union and the perceived threat of Communist expansion in East Asia, Communist-backed labour strikes in 1947 and 1948, and the Korean War (1950–53) persuaded SCAP to reconsider many of its intended reforms in order to cultivate an economically strong and politically conservative ally in the Pacific, where it could base its military operations and hardware. The San Francisco Peace Treaty, signed on 8 September 1951 between Japan and 49 countries, officially ended the war, divesting Japan of occupied territories and confiscating Japan's foreign assets. The US–Japan Security Treaty signed a month later ensured an economic and military alliance between Japan and the United States.

While SCAP executed and purged some of the wartime government officials, it also reinstated former ministry officials to manage Japan's economic and industrial recovery, thereby preserving Japan's pre-war institutions and economic system. The nature of bureaucratic rule and the character of the bureaucracy remained intact because the officials who planned Japan's post-war industrial recovery were former officers of MCI and MOF. Nine former officials from MOF assumed upper-management positions in MOF. Forty-two officials from the Ministry of Munitions took upper-management positions in MCI, which was re-established in 1946, and then in the

Ministry of International Trade and Industry (MITI), which was formed through the consolidation of MCI and the Board of Trade in 1949. As an example, officials who served in the General Affairs Bureau in MCI in the 1930s, including Yamamoto Takayuki and Hirai Tomisaburo, Yoshida Tenjiro, Ishihara Takeo and Tokunaga Hisatsugu, became MITI Vice-Ministers in the 1950s and 1960s.[3] They planned Japan's initial post-war industrial policy while maintaining a close relationship with their former colleagues in MCI. SCAP staff's ignorance of the Japanese language and social system compelled them to rely on existing institutions, namely the bureaucracy, to implement reform policies. After SCAP's exit from Japan, these institutions continued to operate, possessing more power than they had before the war.[4]

It was a double-edged sword. The bureaucrats who had run the war effort were deeply humiliated by Japan's defeat and the subsequent occupation by the United States. Refusing to capitulate spiritually to American Occupation, they worked vigorously to plan and implement policy that would revive Japan's devastated economy. Japan rising from the ashes of defeat and overtaking the United States on the economic front would demonstrate to the world that Japan was a power to be reckoned with. However, the officials' loyalty to their ministries and the ministries' reticence to release control of their administrative territories and deregulate markets created a rigidity and insularity in the administrative system. The rigidity of the system was exacerbated by the consistent support of ministerial policies by the National Diet and by the Japanese people who believed that Japan's success in global markets was the consequence of the policies of the elite ministerial officials and that the bureaucracy was impervious to failure. Only a minority of Japanese questioned the wisdom of these policies.

The main *zaibatsu* that were operating during the war were Sumitomo, Mitsui, Mitsubishi, Yasuda, Furukawa, Nissan, Okura and Nomura. SCAP first dissolved the holding companies[5] so that the family owners no longer held the controlling interest. The 'economic purge' of the executives who had directed the companies during the war was delayed until January 1947, when ultimately 1400 executives were retired. The Mitsubishi and Mitsui trading companies were dismantled in July 1947, but out of the 325 companies slated for liquidation only 18 were actually split up because the Cold War and the fear of Communist expansion convinced SCAP to reverse its initial stand and follow a more lenient course, allowing the combines to join with the ministries, mainly MITI and MOF, to rebuild the economy.

The reforms of the *zaibatsu* were negligible because the *zaibatsu* reorganized into groups of enterprises (*keiretsu*) and the *zaibatsu*'s main banks were at the centre of the capitalization. The financial groups that funded the domestic economy included Mitsui, Mitsubishi and Sumitomo. Centred on one bank ('main bank') that funded corporate investment, the conglomerates had cross-shareholdings and directors in common. Smaller firms were on extended contracts to supply parts and services. The small firms were partially owned by a conglomerate and produced parts solely for one *keiretsu*. They were known as 'first-tier' suppliers. The 'second-tier' and 'third-tier' firms were contracted to supply smaller amounts and produced for other enterprises as well. Many of these firms had supplied parts for the *zaibatsu* during the war.

Japan's economy was helped considerably by the Korean War. Through the production of munitions for America's military, Japan's exports increased by 26 per cent.

The Bank of Japan initially controlled the net additional lending of metropolitan banks, and by 1957 of regional banks, dictating to each bank quarterly the amount acceptable through the extra-legal policy tool 'window guidance' (*madoguchi shido*). The BOJ decided the quotas according to the ranking of the banks from the metropolitan banks down to the regional banks. The state banks were also ranked. The IBJ was ranked first, while the Long-Term Credit Bank and Nippon Credit Bank were ranked second and third respectively.[6] Banks adhered to the dictates because through this policy, they could achieve an equal market share and simultaneously be protected by the BOJ, as the lender of last resort, and by MOF, the ministry that protected the banks against losses. 'Window guidance' was formally abolished in the early 1990s.

The Anti-Monopoly Law was enacted in 1947, but was relaxed by 1953 to allow the financial companies within each oligopoly to own as much as 10 per cent of the shares of the firms not connected to finance.[7] In order to increase production capacity, MITI's Industrial Rationalization Council requested that the oligopolies invest capital in domestic firms.

Japanese-style democracy: a one-party system

The Liberal Democratic Party (LDP) has dominated Japanese politics since 1955, hence the term '1955 political system'.[8] Previously, it was stated that for a brief three-year break, 1993–96, LDP politicians made an exodus from the party to form several parties in order to initiate reforms of the political system and policies that would stimulate Japan's flagging economy. However, the LDP returned in force in 1996 to dominate the political arena as Japan's economic woes continued.

In most Western countries, no single political party has been in power long enough to give bureaucrats the consistent support to draft laws and implement policies nor are there democratic societies where ministries can operate unfettered by legal sanction as they operate in Japan. There are three key reasons for this unwavering political support. The first is that Japan's political economic system can be described as pork-barrel and protectionist. Big business and business federations make large contributions to LDP coffers. The LDP gets votes and large donations from traditional support groups, such as small local firms and from businesses engaged in construction, transportation and telecommunications, in exchange for contracts for public works projects.

The second reason is that the LDP receives substantial support from special interest groups represented by the ministries *vis-à-vis* associations and federations.

The third is related to the network of bureaucrats throughout Japan's socio-political system. Bureaucrats traditionally have sought political office in both national and local government Diets on the LDP ticket. A recent example is the snap elections that former Prime Minister Koizumi called in August 2005 when his bill for the privatization of Japan Posts was initially voted down in the Lower House. He recruited Katayuki Satsuki, a female official in the Ministry of Finance (a ministry with which he remained on good terms) to run on the LDP ticket and won a seat in the Lower House. Katayuki entered MOF in 1982 as an elite career officer, achieving a number of influential positions in the ministry, including Director of the Policy Evaluation office, overall Coordination Division in the Minister's Secretariat in 2000, and Director for Legal Affairs in the Budget Bureau in 2004. Katayuki began her term in 2005 as the Parliamentary

Secretary for Economy, Trade and Industry. Ninety-four former government officials ran for the September 2005 elections (57 on the LDP ticket and 25 on the DPJ ticket).[9]

Former MCI official Kishi Nobuske, Japan's prime minister from 1957–60, is credited with being the father of the LDP and the kingpin of the 1955 political system. His career illustrates explicitly how SCAP's 'reverse reforms' policy effectively perpetuated Japan's wartime government administration of the economy and further enhanced the power of the bureaucracy.

Kishi was arrested in 1945 and imprisoned as a suspected Class A war criminal. While he was imprisoned, he planned tactics that would lead a right-wing political party to power, a party he established in 1944 as 'The Kishi New Party' (*Kishi Shinto*). Although Tojo and other top officials were tried and executed, Kishi was purged and forbidden to assume a public post. However, due to SCAP's paranoia regarding Communist expansion in the Pacific, the order was rescinded and Kishi entered the political arena and joined the ultra-conservative Japan Democratic Party.

Although he had substantial financial backing from business when he entered politics, he tried to build the party he had envisioned in prison with politicians who were members of a pre-war conservative party and bureaucrats. In his fine chronicle of Kishi's ascent to prime minister, Richard J. Samuels maintained that Kishi's right-wing party was intent on revising the new constitution and the security treaty to allow Japan to rearm in order to defend itself.

Despite ideological differences with the other main conservative party, the Liberal Party whose president was Prime Minister Yoshida Shigeru, the determined Kishi was able to form the ultra-conservative Liberal Democratic Party. Kishi became the party's president and the prime minister in 1957. Kishi was a master politician and shrewdly used the United States' paranoia of communist expansion to his advantage to push his conservative ideology and policies.[10]

The United States was instrumental in guaranteeing that LDP politicians would dominate the National Diet in the first election to ensure a conservative government. All Communist-backed labour union protests were quashed. Also, the CIA funnelled money to the LDP in the 1950s and 1960s. The CIA had created a fund, known as the 'M-Fund', that was organized from the sale of Japanese military supplies left over from the war. The US State Department announced in July 2006 that, although these payments were stopped by President Lyndon Johnson in 1964, payments for 'covert programs of propaganda and social action to encourage Japanese to reject the influence of the left' continued until 1968.[11]

Kishi's determination to renew the United States–Japan Security Treaty in 1960, despite public protests and violent demonstrations, forced his resignation in that year. Abe Shinzo argued in *Toward a Beautiful Country* that the chronicles about those turbulent days were misleading. He contended that the initial 1951 treaty inhibited the Japanese from prosecuting Americans who perpetrated crimes in Japan (e.g., military personnel) but that his grandfather negotiated a revised treaty that gave Japan more autonomy from the United States and gave the Japanese more power to prosecute.

Japan's ultra-conservatism, pork-barrel and protectionist policies remain a constant reminder of what American policies for post-war reconstruction wrought:

1. Continuation of Japan's administrative system with the reinstatement of former MCI and MOF officials to manage Japan's economic recovery.
2. Support of ministerial policies from the conservative LDP.
3. Oligopolies were left relatively intact in order to promote a speedy economic recovery.
4. Intensification of interpersonal ties between government and big business.

The Industrial Bank of Japan (IBJ) assumed an even more important role than it had played during the war. A Special Corporation operated by MITI and MOF, the IBJ funded firms in an all out effort to win the economic war. By 1966, Japan's current account balance was in the black.

Between1955 and 1973, Japanese GDP had increased almost six times and Japan, as stated earlier, had achieved the rank of third largest economy in the world, following the United States and the Soviet Union. The policies of the economic ministries, MITI and MOF are considered the drivers of this rapid economic growth. Nevertheless, it is difficult to analyse quantitatively the extent to which ministerial policy actually drove the economy. Besides SCAP's 'reverse reforms', a number of other major factors must be considered:

1. A cheap currency until 1971 (¥360 per dollar).
2. Access to cheap technologies.
3. Anti-monopoly legislation allowing MITI to form cartels, to control retail pricing and to sanction cross-shareholdings.
4. High savings rates.
5. America's willingness to open markets to the surge of Japanese exports in order to maintain a strong alliance in the Pacific.
6. SCAP's purge of Communist sympathizers and the quelling of labour strikes to ensure a stable workforce and an environment for economic recovery.
7. 1964 Tokyo Olympics that marked a spurt in infrastructure construction and industrial development.
8. Consistent support for industrial and economic policies from both the National Diet and business.

Ministerial policies 1971: the system continues

A series of external shocks significantly affected MITI's long-term policies.

The first shock was the collapse in 1971 of the Bretton Woods System of fixed exchange rates and the end of the gold standard on which currencies' values were based. In the early 1970s, the Vietnam War caused a rapid rise in inflation and the United States experienced a trade deficit for the first time in the twentieth century. The US dollar that had been valued at $35 per ounce of gold was weakened by America's inability to cut spending and reduce its trade deficit. As the government printed more money to fund operations in Vietnam, America's gold coverage of the dollar dropped to 11 per cent and in August 1971,[12] President Nixon imposed a 90-day wage and price controls as well as a 10 per cent import surcharge. The so-called 'Nixon shock' effectively made the dollar inconvertible directly to gold, except on the open markets. Even though the import surcharge was dropped five months later, there was a general revaluation of currencies. By 1976 there was no longer a fixed exchange rate.

The revaluation of currencies was a jolt to Japanese economists because the yen had been set for 22 years at ¥360 per dollar, allowing Japanese exports to flood foreign markets. MOF officials reacted by suppressing the yen to only ¥300 so that prices of exports in the American market were relatively unaffected. They felt that as long as Japan ran a trade surplus with the United States, they were in control of the economy and their administrative territory. Japan continued to hoard dollars in the United States and, indeed, this policy remains implicit to the economic ministries' mercantile mind-set.

Ministerial policies 1974–: the system continues

The second external shock to MITI and MOF's policies was the 'oil shock' in December 1973 that increased the price of petroleum and strengthened the yen to ¥260 per dollar. MITI's industrial policy had encompassed the development of the petrol-chemical industry, since the Japanese must import 99 per cent of its fossil fuels. But MITI's long-term plans to develop petrol-chemicals and other energy-intensive industries such as aluminium and plastics were thwarted. In order to deal with problems developing from structurally damaged energy intensive industries and the ensuing four-year recession, the ministry continued to use 'administrative guidance' to form anti-recession cartels. The anti-recession cartel policies, policies that had been implemented during Japan's period of rapid economic growth, continue for industries such as steel under the Structurally Depressed Industry Law as well as for the construction industry.

Although MITI's revised its industrial policy to focus on information systems, the ministries resolutely maintained administrative jurisdiction over their industrial sectors and continued planning and implementing mercantile and protectionist policies. The policies included doling out subsidies to the depressed energy-intensive industries. The US trade policies with Japan as a most favoured nation and its open markets to Japanese goods gave the economic ministries little incentive to revise the policies.

Recession cartels played a primary role in limiting competition from foreign manufacturers. Yamamura Kozo maintained that the recession cartel policy was merely a continuation of the policies that had promoted rapid economic growth and that the management of capital investment, while reducing risks through the use of cartels, was no longer productive.[13] The LDP supported MITI's policies because politicians needed contributions from businesses for their campaign coffers. Yamamura also contended that the continuation of these policies benefited MITI officials as well:

> The LDP was understandably anxious to accommodate the wishes of the industry since the later provided virtually all of the LDP's political funds... some high-ranking MITI officers had an incentive to be more helpful to the largest firms that had invited them to fill high managerial posts after their retirement.[14]

Mikuni Akio is the president of a Japanese investor-supported bond-ratio agency and a former executive of Nomura Securities, Co. He has criticized the bureaucracy's policies in an array of commentaries and books. In 1998, he wrote about the role that industrial associations played in the formation of cartels, as they had during the 1930s:

> These industrial associations and the implied promise of government intervention had helped maintain the viability of member companies, thus obviating the need for individual companies to accumulate the sufficient capital on their own to withstand downturns. Anti-trust laws do exist, but they are largely empty.[15,16]

Despite these set-backs and a slow-down in economic growth, Japan achieved the position of the second largest economy in the world behind the United States by the 1980s. Mercantile and protectionist policies continued throughout the 1980s and 1990s. Mikuni contended that Japan's economic problems were caused primarily by mercantile policies. He and R. Taggart Murphy wrote in 2003, when Japan was the largest creditor in the world with the largest trade surplus:

> A mercantile regime may enjoy a period of success as it accumulates specie – or, in today's terms, claims on other countries. But it usually runs into some kind of monetary train wreck. The mercantilist's efforts to convert its claims on others into its own

currency drive up the exchange rate because foreigners, whose sales to the mercantilist country are restricted, have few ways of accumulating the mercantilist's currency in the first place, so little of its currency is held outside its borders. The mercantilist exporters then find that no one can afford to buy their goods.[17]

Mikuni warned in 2006 that Japan's economy was mainly supported by exports of cars and electronics to the United States:

A reduction of exports is not the only problem. A decline in US consumption leads to a surplus of dollars. And as the value of the dollar declines, the yen gets stronger.[18]

The appreciation of the yen to ¥99 per dollar in March 2008 pressured Japanese car manufacturers to consider ways to prevent the erosion of their share of the American market, their largest by far. Mizuno Tatsuya, an analyst at Fitch, the Tokyo rating firm, told the *Financial Times* that Toyota was 50 per cent dependent on the United States and Honda was 60–70 per cent dependent on American buyers. If the yen rose by only ¥1 per dollar, Toyota's operating profits would fall ¥35 billion and Honda's would fall ¥20 billion. When the yen appreciated in the 1990s, the automobile industry cut costs and moved production to North America.[19] Even though the producer's exports to emerging markets has reduced some of the dependence on the major economies, a global economic down-turn and competition from domestic car manufacturers would hamper Toyota and Honda from realizing long-term supremacy in the global market-place.

Sony, the electronics and media giant, suffered a sizable decrease in profits not only because of the weak dollar, but also because of the yen's rise against the euro. Turbulent exchange rates and a slumping Nikkei, which affected the value of its financial component, in 2007 reduced Sony's prediction of ¥450 billion operating profits to ¥410 for the financial year.[20] Sony had based its estimated operating profits on ¥105 per dollar in December. However, the yen's further appreciation portended that Sony's operating profits could be cut by more than ¥30 billion. Mizuno warned that the yen's appreciation would have an even bigger effect on Sony in fiscal 2008.[21]

Japanese initially blamed the United States and the end of the Cold War in 1989 for the recession rather than the bureaucracy which had forged mercantile policies throughout the post-war years. But the continuing reticence of the ministries to abandon mercantile policies and to deregulate markets more rapidly effectively sustained the intimate relationship between business and the bureaucracy.

4
Amakudari: The Ties that Bind the Bureaucracy with the Private and Public Sectors and Politics

> There can be no doubt that the need for post-retirement *amakudari* has weakened the overall independence of the Japanese civil service. There can also be no doubt that over time, the continued practice of *amakudari* contributed to serious corruption as was revealed in 1993, in the bribery and bid-rigging scandals throughout the construction industry.
>
> (Johnson, 1995)[1]

Western media in the 1980s used the term 'Japan Inc.' to describe the intimate relationship between the bureaucracy, politicians and big business, which was assumed to be the core component of Japan's success in global markets. When the asset inflated bubble burst in 1990 and the attempts by government to reignite a recessive economy through the release of successive fiscal stimulus packages did little more than to drain public revenue, 'Japan, Inc.' was no longer considered to be the ideal model to copy. Politicians' efforts to initiate structural reforms of the administrative system were frustrated by the key players in the political economy; the bureaucracy, business and political parties who had numerous vested interests.

Pork-barrel politics is a principal characteristic of the administrative system. Both large and small businesses rely heavily on the appropriation of government funds for public works and contribute large sums to political party coffers, particularly to the LDP. The LDP has traditionally supported ministerial policies and, consequently, this relationship has served to rigidify the system of management of the political economy. The sections in Chapter 1 regarding reforms of the Japan Highway Corporation and the Post Office serve to illustrate this characteristic.

The national ministries extend controls over the political economy through mechanisms that are invariably implemented or enhanced by the *amakudari* system. It began in the 1930s when the government started to strictly regulate the economy for the war effort. Business owners employed bureaucrats in order to determine future government directives as well as lobby interests. The system benefits officials, who retire earlier than staff in the private sector, usually between the ages of 57 and 60, stepping aside for the younger officials intent on promotion. The ministries want to provide a new source of income that enhances pensions, which is not as high as in the private sector.

The system provides an incentive for officers who would otherwise seek employment in the private sector rather than the civil service, where salaries are not as lucrative. However, the system also serves the interests of the ministries and their former colleagues throughout the public and private sectors and increases the bureaucracy's power to control the implementation of economic and industrial policies. *Amakudari* expedites the use of such policy tools as 'administrative guidance', which will be explained later in this chapter. The relationship between a bureaucrat and a former colleague who is posted in businesses in a sector under their ministry's administrative jurisdiction automatically tightens the ministry's grip on that sector. Originally, the elite bureaucrats were the main beneficiaries of *amakudari* but, gradually, officers in middle management as well as non-career officers were also included in the system.

The National Employment Agency actively seeks upper-management positions in the private sector for retiring ministry officials, but the ministries also search on behalf of their staff, usually in companies in the sectors they administrate. As an example, MOF officials find employment in the financial industry, while METI officials find employment in the manufacturing and retail industries. However, ministry officials can be placed directly upon retirement in corporations that are not directly within their ministry's administrative jurisdiction.

Ministerial manipulation of *amakudari* in Special Corporations/IAIs

Yokosuberi or 'side-slipping' refers to bureaucrats entering Special Corporations/ IAIs before migrating to the private sector. There are various ways that ministries can manipulate the *amakudari* system through the shrewd use of these organizations:

1. If retired bureaucrats are on the staff of two organizations simultaneously (for example, advisors and board members), they can receive two salaries plus ministry benefits.
2. There are instances where bureaucrats are sent by their ministries to work in associations and in Special Corporations/IAIs while they are still engaged by their ministries (and drawing a salary). They then migrate to the private sector without waiting out the two-year period of grace.
3. Another option for bureaucrats is to remain attached in some way to Special Corporations/IAIs through their subsidiaries (as advisors or members of boards) while working for private businesses, and receiving salaries from both employers.
4. The period of stay in Special Corporations/IAIs is usually two years because positions are much sought after. However, there are instances where periods of stay can be as long as six years.[2]
5. Positions in Special Corporations/IAIs may be given to elite bureaucrats who have not reached retirement age, but are considered to be nearing the end of their careers. The 'gift' is actually a sign to officials that they will not be promoted much higher in their ministries, but their loyalty is appreciated. The substantial salaries that top management receives make Special Corporations/ IAIs particularly enticing to officials. They may remain longer if they cannot find employment elsewhere.

The term 'retired' refers to bureaucrats who are within ten years of retiring from their ministries.

The ministries can also 'loan' officials to Special Corporations/ IAIs. Known as *shukko* ('on loan to another company'), the temporary postings can be from one to three years. Although the officials are still connected to their ministries, they are identified as officers of the organizations where they have been transferred. And while the posts are considered to be temporary, they can develop into permanent positions. Essentially, *shukko* can be the catalyst for *amakudari*.

A survey released by the Lower House in March 2007 revealed the number of Special Corporations/IAIs (including subsidiaries) maintained by ministries and the number of retired bureaucrats, including employees on loan to these entities:

1. The Ministry of Land, Infrastructure and Transport: 834 entities, 6386 bureaucrats.
2. Ministry of Health, Labour and Welfare: 709 entities, 4007 former officials.
3. Defence Ministry: 207 entities, 3917 former employees.
4. Ministry of Education, Culture, Sports, Science and Technology: 934 entities, 3007 former ministry officials[3]

The central ministries can also extend control over local government policies by 'loaning' officials to local governments to provide 'guidance' in planning local policies. The officials can serve for periods up to three years and are a direct pipeline to their ministries, conveying information about local government activities and whether the policies have been implemented according to the ministries' 'guidance.'

Conversely, local government officers are 'loaned' to central ministries to relay information regarding their regions' needs, in the hope that the local government will be granted subsidies for health, education and public works.

Amakudari to research institutes

The ministries operate research institutes where officials are 'loaned' for a two-year period of grace before migrating to the private sector. Commonly, administrative vice-ministers gain permanent positions in these organizations, many of which are funded by the ministries' Special Corporations/IAIs. As an example, METI's Industrial Policy Research Institute is supported by METI's Special Corporation, the Japan Corporation for the Promotion of Bicycle Racing and the Japan Racing Association (Japan Keiren Association).

Amakudari to central government advisory panels

The *Asahi News* conducted a survey on the number of retired bureaucrats on regular central government advisory panels at the beginning of 2005. On 4 February, it reported that out of 108 advisory panels, 15 have regular members: 42.2 per cent of those members were former bureaucrats, receiving a monthly salary of ¥1.146 million. The panel chair receives ¥1.301 million. Many of the former bureaucrats sit on panels that deal with grievances from the public and from businesses. The survey tallied that out of the six members of the Labor Insurance Appeal Committee who decided on applications for workers' compensation insurance, four were former ministry officials. Some bureaucrats chair panels that are under their former ministries and agencies administrative jurisdiction.[4]

Amakudari to public office

Japanese political dynamics belie the 'Japan Inc.' image that there is consensus and cooperation among politicians and bureaucrats. The national ministries write about 86 per cent of all legislation and are at the spearhead of implementing laws. Politicians, particularly prime ministers like Koizumi, have attempted to expand the influence of the executive office, but with little success. And despite the efforts of Abe and Fukuda to whittle away power from the ministries, the bureaucracy still rules.

Elite ministerial officials seek elected office after retirement, mainly on the LDP ticket. Traditionally, many governors, vice-governors and members of both Houses in the National Diet have been migrating officials from the bureaucracy. But the former officials will remain loyal to their ministries and support policies. Indeed, former officials who are governors will court their former colleagues for subsidies and contracts for public works projects. In return, they follow ministerial guidance regarding the planning of local policies. This is particularly true in the less affluent prefectures that are beholden to central government.

As an example, Ehime Prefecture is a rural prefecture on the island of Shikoku that generates only about 36 per cent local taxes. When Moriyuki Kato was elected to the office of governor in 1999, local business owners expressed the hope that since Kato was a former high-ranking official in the Ministry of Education, he would be a good link to the national ministries and facilitate the procurement of public works contracts and subsidies. But by 2002, local sentiment was not as positive.

The controversial history textbook edited by the ministries was distributed to schools throughout Japan in 2001. Governor Kato, a proponent of the textbook that glosses over Japan's wartime atrocities in Asia, publicly announced in 2002 that he felt that the book '...is the most appropriate to deepen people's appreciation of the history of the country'. Although many local citizens were opposed to the textbook, Kato received more support from Abe on 15 May 2004 at an Ehime Town meeting for the revised education bill.[5] The hall was stuffed with 100 educators with links to Kato's former ministry. A subsequent investigation of the event revealed the following November that 65 educators were paid ¥5,000 each for attending and that one member was given the task of spouting statements in support of the textbooks and asking questions prepared by the ministry. Despite the revelation that the Town Hall meeting was rigged and a lawsuit was filed in December 2005 against Kato by 1000 people (including Ehime residents, South Koreans and Chinese) demanding that the book not be introduced in four prefectural schools, the controversial textbook was distributed to the schools in April 2006.[6]

In October 2006 when central government requested that Ehime host a nuclear reactor that used plutonium mix fuel, despite vehement protests from civic groups, Kato welcomed the project since Ehime would undoubtedly benefit from substantial government subsidies.[7]

Amakudari to the private sector

A big incentive drawing Japanese to careers in the national ministries are the positions in upper management in private corporations and the comfortable salary that they receive simultaneously with their pensions from the ministries. The two years of service or *yokosuberi* in Special Corporations/IAIs is beneficial to officials because they can make contacts to future employers if they have not already done so during their time in the ministries. Foreign firms entering the Japanese market hire former officials in order to promote interests to government. Kent Calder maintained in 1989 that a large number of retired bureaucrats were executives in the subsidiaries of foreign multinationals in the 1980s. He gave the example of IBM Japan, which hired officials from MOF, the BOJ and the Science and Technology Agency. In the late 1980s, IBM employed three elite MITI officials because it wanted to enter the information service businesses sector and Fujitsu, a domestic company that had been raised by MITI, had become the largest computer manufacturer in 1979. Calder contended:

Counting its three senior ex-MITI officials, IBM Japan's personnel roster throughout the early and mid-1980s included more retired senior bureaucrats than any domestic Japanese computer producer.[8,9,10]

Amakudari and 'administrative guidance'

The use of the policy tool 'administrative guidance' (gyoseishido) is indicative of the Japanese system of ministerial administration over industrial sectors and is commonly implemented by officials who have connections with the businesses that are under their ministries administrative jurisdiction.

MITI began using 'administrative guidance' in 1952 in order to form cartels of industries considered important to national interests, such as heavy industries and petrochemicals, protecting them from foreign competition. It was previously explained that the Anti-Monopoly Law was passed in 1947. However, it was later revised in the early 1950s to allow the formation of cartels.

Companies will usually receive notification requesting that they follow ministerial regulation. The directives are transmitted usually in writing or by telephone (although a law in 1997 formally curtailed the use of a telephone) but also in person when bureaucrats meet with members of industrial associations whose companies are under the administrative jurisdiction of the bureaucrats' ministries. Companies rarely reject guidance for a number of reasons, but a primary factor that promotes acquiescence to elite authority is the fear of future retribution, in such forms as fines, and the rejection of permits and applications for patents and subsidies for R&D. Furthermore, METI administrates the distribution of fossil fuels and other natural resources vital to manufacturers and has the power to designate the route of distribution to companies. Businessmen who are members of industrial associations are also concerned that if they alone choose to break ranks with fellow members who comply with the directives, they may face a boycott of their goods by the majority.

Amakudari and 'window guidance': non-performing loans

During the 1990s a number of scandals linking the failures of financial institutions with MOF officials in the regulatory agency that monitored the *keiretsu* main banks and other financial institutions were covered extensively by the Japanese media. When the inflated price of land began to fall in 1991 followed by a drop in stock prices in 1992, a number of corporate borrowers defaulted on their loans. In 1993, relatively small financial institutions failed, but their equities were purchased by solvent banks. However, when housing loan companies (*jusen*) failed in 1995, financial institutions that served agricultural cooperatives were caught with a heavy load of bad loans. Farmers pressured their representatives in the Diet to vote for a bill calling for the injection of ¥685 billion of public funds into the financial institutions. The action was widely covered by media and brought public outrage.

The failure in 1996–97 of Sanyo Securities Co, Hokkaido Takushoku Bank and Yamaichi Securities, three major financial institutions, followed in 1998 by the Nippon Credit Bank (NCB) and the Long-Term Credit Bank (LTCB), both Special Corporations that had been established in the 1950s by MOF, revealed the severity of the non-performing loan problem. Non-performing loans (NPL) are loans that are not accruing interest. During the 1990s the government injected ¥9,000 billion ($83.5 billion) into banks in order to avoid a banking crisis.[11]

The Japan Economic Institute, an organization operated under the auspices of the Ministry of Foreign Affairs, reported in August 2000 that the Financial Services Agency declared that the amount of problem loans for all banks as of March 2000 equalled ¥81.8 trillion ($743.6 billion at ¥110 = $1.00) compared with ¥80.6 billion in 1998.[12]

The scandal in 1997 surrounding the entertainment of MOF and BOJ officials at expensive restaurants and clubs by banks brought to public attention that the non-disclosure of NPL by the banks was partially the consequence of the intimate relationship between the BOJ, MOF and the banks that had been promoted through the *amakudari* system. In their defence, the banks insisted that they had been pressured by the officials to provide the entertainment. Many retired bureaucrats from MOF and retired executives are employed in top management positions in metropolitan banks and financial institutions. As of 1992, there were 78 former MOF officials and 64 BOJ officers on the boards of 115 listed banks: 51 per cent of the banks were employing former MOF officials on their boards, 44 per cent had former BOJ executives on their boards, and 69 per cent had an official from either MOF or the BOJ.[13]

Until the 1990s, all Japanese banks regarded both the BOJ and MOF regulators as their protectors who shielded them from close scrutiny by outside auditors. Richard Werner described how the extra-legal policy tool *'window guidance'* could pressure banks to hire retired officials. He referred to an incident which involved a bank in Nagoya which dismissed a BOJ *amakudari* official. The dismissal was considered a form of 'misbehavior'. The BOJ would 'punish' banks by reducing loan quotas, which evidently happened frequently.[14]

Edward Lincoln claimed in 2003 that, although government estimates of the amount of NPL at the end of September 2002 were ¥40 trillion ($330 billion) and that during the decade 1993–2003 the banks had written off ¥83 trillion (about $700 billion) of NPL, there was speculation in the private sector that the 'real amount' of loans that had been written off did not necessarily represent the loans that were resolved. In many cases, the banks simply set aside reserves equal to the amount of the loan while taking no action against the borrower to recover collateral, leaving 'zombie' borrowers effectively bankrupt but still in business.[15]

Two examples of poor screening practices and regulatory procedures that are related to *amakudari* are the Industrial Bank of Japan (IBJ) and Shin Ginko, a bank established by the Tokyo Metropolitan Government in 2005.

NPL: the (IBJ)

An example of *amakudari* of an official from the IBJ to a corporation that effectively went bankrupt, triggering the demise of the IBJ, is the case of Sogo Company, a department store chain. When the store collapsed in April 2002, it owed ¥13.6 billion to the IBJ, its main bank.[16] IBJ president Nishimura Masao testified before the Diet that even though the IBJ knew that Sogo was insolvent, it continued to loan substantial sums. Mikuni and Murphy contended that the IBJ and Sogo were closely associated and that if the IBJ called in loans to Sogo it would be tantamount to admitting publicly that it was in trouble. Furthermore, Sogo's president had held a top position at the IBJ.[17] Sogo's acute distress in the second half of the 1990s and its imminent collapse prompted the government to urge Fuji Bank to purchase IBJ equity in a stock-swap transaction for ¥2.826 trillion ($30.76 billion).[18] In April 2002, Fuji together with the IBJ merged with Dai-ichi Kangyo Bank. The new bank was renamed Mizuho Financial Group.

NPL: Shin Ginko Tokyo

The announcement by Shin Ginko Tokyo in March 2008 that defaults on loans had escalated to ¥28.5 billion indicated that the NPL problem still haunted Japanese financial institutions and that poor regulatory practices were at the root of the problem. Tokyo governor Ishihara Shintaro, a politically powerful and ultra-conservative politician,[19] had promoted its establishment in April 2005 in order to finance small and medium-size businesses with a capital investment of ¥100 billion of tax revenue by the Tokyo metropolitan government. Since then, even though each contract was not to exceed ¥50 million, the bank, alluded to as 'Ishihara Bank', extended loans and loan guarantees totalling ¥240 billion, despite the ¥2.4 billion loan defaults by the end of 2005. By September 2007, Shin Ginko's losses totalled ¥93.6 billion. By December, the bank's NPL has escalated to ¥18 billion or approximately 13 per cent of ¥134.5 billion in loans to SME. Additionally, an in-house probe revealed that 35 of the loans were based on the firms' questionable financial reports and that the clients never intended to repay the loans.[20] The reason given for the defaults was poor screening of the borrowers and poor management.[21] The bank also wasted ¥10.9 billion during the first two years in business in investments related to computerized systems and other operations. In February 2008, Shin Ginko applied to Tokyo Metropolitan Government for an injection of ¥40 billion to counteract the losses.[22] Despite public outrage, a Tokyo Metropolitan

Assembly panel approved the request with the stipulation that the funding would be the final bailout using tax revenue.[23]

The bureaucracy and bid-rigging: Special Corporations/IAI's at the centre

Merely changing the name of Special Corporations to Independent Administrative Institutions and merging some of the bankrupt Special Corporations with solvent ones did little to stop wasteful spending of tax revenue or the migration of bureaucrats into IAIs.

The *amakudari* system is a breeding ground for bid-rigging activities and collusion among bureaucrats and businessmen. The ministries' Special Corporations/IAIs grant government contracts for public works projects to private industries and Special Corporations/IAIs are the vehicles that connect the ministries to these industries. Former bureaucrats can choose the recipients of the lucrative contracts that are funded by tax revenue, and in return receive lucrative employment in the corporations to whom they have awarded contracts. The Lower House survey showed that in 2006 alone, of the ¥1.8313 trillion ($17.1 billion) in disbursement for state projects, 98 per cent (¥1.8001 trillion) was contracted to those entities without bidding procedures.

The secretariat of the Cabinet's Headquarters for Administrative Reform on 8 November 2007 released documents to a government panel of experts on streamlining public corporations. Originally, 57 corporations were set up to take over part of the operations of the ministries and agencies but this number has increased to 101, a similar pattern to that which evolved as the ministries were establishing their Special Corporations The report showed that 40 out of 101 Special Corporations/IAIs awarded contracts to their subsidiaries with more than 90 per cent of the contracts completed without competitive bidding. The documents also revealed that the 101 Special Corporations/IAIs had altogether 236 affiliates. Companies where one-third or more of their posts were occupied by former directors and senior officials of the IAIs were among the affiliates. Also, 230 former officials at the 101 corporations had assumed director's posts at affiliates in fiscal 2005 through *amakudari*.[24]

In December 2006, reacting to reports of bid-rigging by local govern-ment officials together with bureaucrats in Special Corporations/IAIs, a revised law was enacted by government that would bring stiff punishment to officials in these corporations who are convicted of involvement in bid-rigging. The revised law included officials in the expressway corporations that were the result of the privatization of the Japan Highway Corporation. Even though an anti-collusion bill was implemented in 2003 to prevent bureaucrats from positively influenc-ing the outcome of bids from corporations, collusion is still prolific.

An incident that clearly illustrates how *amakudari* connects Special Corporations/IAIs with the private sector in encouraging bid-rigging occurred in April 2007 when five corporations were raided for rigging bids for projects ordered by the Japan Green Resources Agency. The agency was known until October 2003 as the Japan Green Resources Corporation, which was established by the Ministry of Agriculture, Forestry and Fisheries.

The five entities as of 2005 had hired 256 former bureaucrats through *amakudari*: 41 of the 44 executive posts were former offi-cials of the Forestry Agency. Japan Forestry Foundation, adminis-trated by the Forestry Agency, had accepted, as of April 2005, 138 bureaucrats, including the chairman who was the former head of the Forestry Agency. Japan Forest Engineering Consultants hired 45 bureaucrats, Japan Forest Technology Association hired 40, and the Japan Federation of Forestry Civil Engineering Research Institute employed 24. According to the investigation by the Japan Fair Trade Commission, the Forestry Agency officials were instrumental in introducing its staff to firms in the private sector. The five entities were among the contractors of Japan Green Resources which were raided by the JFTC.[25] In May 2007 Agriculture Minister Matsuoka Toshikatsu who was under investigation for allegedly receiving political donations from Japan Green Resources contractors com-mitted suicide. A few days later, Yamazaki Shinichi, the former head of the agency whose home was searched by Tokyo District Special Prosecutors Office, also committed suicide.

The post-war system sustained

Amakudari remains an 'entrenched' institution as the Japanese continue to defer to ministerial authority. The system has survived for over 60 years, even though it has perpetuated a corruption that has become an integral part of the system of administration. In January 2006, a government report announced that in December 2005, 34 per cent of senior bureaucrats who had retired from their ministries as of August had taken jobs in government affiliates.

Since 2006, government has released a number of proposals to restrict *amakudari*. The Ministry of Internal Affairs and Communications implemented new rules in August 2006 regarding post-retirement positions for central ministry officials after data revealed in April that 70 per cent of 1968 bureaucrats had been assisted by their ministries and agencies to land jobs for the period 2004 to 2006 in sectors under the administrative jurisdiction of their organizations.

In March 2007, a panel led by Abe submitted a plan that would prohibit the ministries finding post-retirement positions for their officials and would create a new body that would centralize job-hunting for all of the ministries. But it would take at least three years to begin operations after its establishment. Abe's comments at the panel discussion summed up why the curtailing of *amakudari* practices will prove difficult:

> I have said that we have to root out the ministries' somewhat forcible job-hunting tactics that are backed by their budgetary power and authority.

In April, Abe's Cabinet approved a bill that would end *amakudari*. The prime minister touted the bill as the biggest reform of the administrative system in 60 years.[26] The bill was submitted to the Diet in June. Besides opposition to the bill by Abe's LDP colleagues, the opposition parties were also against it, contending that the bill did not guarantee the end of collusion between government and the private sector. Abe's coalition government, frustrated by the opposition, temporarily withdrew the bill through the Diet.

Nevertheless, the struggle to eradicate *amakudari* continued a year later in April 2008, when Fukuda's administration announced that a draft bill for further reform and regulation of 101 Special Corporations/IAIs will be submitted to the Diet. If passed, the bill would be law in 2010. Applicants from outside the ministries would be able to apply for positions in the ministries' organizations, but appointments would be approved by all members of the cabinet.

Also, retired bureaucrats working in IAIs would be prohibited from side-slipping into businesses that have connections with the organizations. However, opponents are sceptical that the new law would act to eliminate *amakudari* since traditionally, the Cabinet has systematically approved the appointments of senior ministry officials to positions in IAIs.[27]

The following chapter describes the institutional factors that facilitate collusion between government and the private sector.

5
Interpersonal Networks in the 'Ruling Triad'

> In upper levels of society, the kone multiply to form whole networks of special relationships. These may derive from one-time favours, school ties or shared experiences, or may involve intricate mutual back-scratching deals.
>
> (van Wolferen, 1990)[1]

'Kone' is a term used by the Japanese to refer to personal connections. The bond between bureaucracy, big business and politicians is fashioned from elaborate networks of formal and informal relationships (e.g., connections) between the three bodies, and generates an ideal environment for ministerial control over Japan's political economy. The networks are forged though mutual obligation (e.g., 'back-scratching') and plays a far more important role than does the 'old boys' network in Western countries.

However, there is another side to this relationship. There is a palpable concern among business owners that they may antagonize the administrators if they do not follow the prescribed guidance and that they will suffer retribution in some form. More importantly, there is an apprehension among members of industrial associations and federations that if they do not comply with the objectives of the majority, they will alienate the other members. Although one key element in the relationship among the 'ruling triad' may be mutual obligation, it must also be emphasized that the relationship may generate mistrust and a prevailing fear of isolation.

Pork-barrel patronage in the prefectures

Pork-barrel politics is a consequence of interpersonal networks in government. Governors strive to create strong links to the central ministries by courting them in various ways, in order to receive subsidies. Local government budgets for entertaining ministry officials (*osettai*) usually depend upon the affluence of the prefectures. Prefectures whose representatives in the national Diet hold Cabinet posts or who are in influential positions in the LDP can forge abiding relationships with business and the bureaucracy. A good example of this type of relationship was reported in the first book (Carpenter, 2003) and is worth mentioning in part here. It also illustrates how expenditures on public works can perpetuate Japan's rising public debt.

Ehime Prefecture is the largest of four prefectures on the island of Shikoku, the smallest of four major islands in the Japanese archipelago. The total population is around 1,500,000 with 500,000 residents in Matsuyama, the capital. The primary industries in this rural area are agriculture (citrus), forestry and fisheries. Secondary industries are shipbuilding, chemicals, machinery and paper pulp. For GDP per capita, Ehime ranks at 35 among the 48 prefectures, 32 for personal income tax, 25 in industrial output, 25 for agricultural produce, and 30 for the size of the budget.[2] Since it is one of the less-endowed prefectures, it is dependent on central government for subsidies.

Iga Sadayuki was Ehime's governor from 1987–99. He was a member of the LDP. As the vice-governor under the previous administration, he was in line to succeed as governor. While he was in office, Iga saw a window of opportunity for accessing large subsidies from the government when, early in his incumbency, Ochi Ehei, Ehime's elected representative to the Lower House in the national Diet, was the Minister of Construction (1988–89) in Prime Minister Takeshita Noboru's first Cabinet.[3] As a consequence, applications for public works projects were accepted in the first Takeshita budget.[4]

Iga continued to cultivate a personal network with MOC, MITI and the Ministry of Agriculture, Forestry and Fisheries officials and was able to access for his constituency more subsidies for public works, which included a network of highways and tunnels, an international airport, a convention centre, modern art museum and the first Foreign Access Zone (FAZ) in Japan. Iga gained a reputation among residents as a governor obsessed with self-glorification.

The Kuroshima Bridge that links Ehime with Hiroshima on the main island of Honshu was a coup for Iga. The bridge was under the management of the Honshu-Shikoku Bridge Authority, the debt-ridden corporation that was one of the entities merged with the Japan Highway Corporation.

Another triumph for the governor was the first Foreign Access Zone (FAZ), which opened in the port city Matsuyama, Ehime's capital in 1993. MITI began to open these installations due to pressure from the United States to open up Japan's markets to more imports. Foreign Access Zones have subsequently been installed throughout Japan, which incorporate distribution centres, exhibition halls and conference rooms and are financed through FILP.

It can be assumed that in the early 1990s, Iga's friends in the ministries considered that the investment in public works projects would be supported by Ehime's expanding economy and would promote small-business growth. A second FAZ was constructed in 1999. The allocation of subsidies also provided lucrative contracts to big businesses and employment to hundreds of workers. Additionally, the ministries had the option of expanding their territory and control in local government by placing branches of their existing public corporations there or by establishing new public corporations. As an example, the Ehime Foreign Access Zone Co. Ltd administered the construction of the first FAZ as well as the second FAZ, building a new port and roads connecting the facilities. METI opened a JETRO branch office in the first FAZ installation to support the promotion of FAZ facilities to foreign investors and business owners.

It is difficult to determine how government intended to use all of the facilities over the long term. Ehime is among a number of prefectures where deflation continues to dominate the economy and local government coffers are empty. The population is also decreasing as residents are moving to more affluent regions to find jobs. The expansion of industry in Ehime is highly unlikely, as companies move production facilities overseas to cut costs. FAZ is not being fully utilized as the facilities are undersubscribed. The exhibition halls remain vacant much of the year. Traffic is relatively light on newly constructed highways and commuters to Hiroshima prefer riding the ferry than crossing the Kurushima Bridge because the tolls are too expensive. The museum is a beautiful structure with luxurious mahogany toilets, but the small collection of art the museum houses questions the justification of the expenditure. It appears that no consideration was given to the ultimate costs of these projects, let alone the drain on local tax revenue for the maintenance of what have come to be known as 'empty boxes.'

The bureaucracy, big business and the LDP

High-ranking bureaucrats meet regularly with party officials and politicians to explain laws and policies they would like implemented, thus encouraging a more intimate relationship between politicians and bureaucrats.

The *Asahi News*, one of Japan's major dailies, discovered in December 2007 that big businesses were among the 109 organizations that had received subsidies from the ministries of economy, trade and industry, land, infrastructure and transport, and agriculture after contributing to the LDP campaign coffers.

The incident illuminates the interpersonal network that continues between Japan's bureaucracy, big business and the LDP: 109 organizations donated ¥780 million in 2006 to the LDP's People's Political Association. The *Asahi News* found that the records of subsidies allocated by the ministries to companies showed that many of the 109 organizations that had made donations in 2006 and were approved for subsidies were automobile manufactures and big companies that engaged in electric power, construction and railway industries. The Political Fund Control Law, enacted in 1994 in an attempt to guarantee transparency in the flow of political contributions, states that organizations cannot contribute to political coffers within a year after subsidies have been granted. However, subsidies for research, surveys and such projects as post-disaster recovery measures are exempt because these subsidies are not connected with special interests.

METI administrates the petroleum industry. The Petroleum Association of Japan, an industrial association whose members are the major oil companies, received ¥4 billion in subsidies during the first half of 2006. The association had contributed ¥80 million to the People's Political Association. The 109 organizations received in total ¥28 billion in subsidies. The 20 largest contributors maintained that they had received the subsidies for non-profit works, but it was discovered that some of the work was connected to condominium development and new business ventures.

The LDP fund-managing official claimed that the confirmation of whether contributors had been the recipients of subsidies was difficult to determine.[5]

The *Asahi News* also exposed donations by 36 organizations, among them major companies in construction, paper and machinery industries, to 24 members in Koizumi, Abe and Fukuda's Cabinet from 2005–06. These companies received ¥7 billion in subsidies from the Ministry of Land, Infrastructure, Transport and Tourism, the Ministry of Economy, Trade and Industry, the Ministry of Agriculture, Forestry and Fisheries, the Environment Ministry and the Defence Ministry. The donations were given to regional LDP branches.

Prime Minister Fukuda and former Prime Minister Abe, who were also recipients of the donations, contended that the donations were proper because the objectives of the subsidies met the conditions for exemptions under the law. They agreed with the LDP fund-managing official's claim that ascertaining the donors who were receiving subsidies would be a difficult task.[6]

The BOJ and the private sector

The former governor of the BOJ, Fukui Toshiko (March 2003 to March 2008) was also implicated in the 1997 scandal concerning the entertainment of MOF and BOJ officials. Fukui, who entered the BOJ in 1958 after graduating with a law degree from Tokyo University, was the deputy governor of the BOJ at the time and, although he was not indicted, he resigned during the investigation and moved to the Fujitsu Research Institute as Chairman in 1998. The institute is said to be a private think-tank, but it engages with METI in numerous joint projects. The senior managing director is METI official Nezu Risaburo, who joined METI in 1984 after graduating from Tokyo University with a law degree.

While Fukui was at Fujitsu Research Institute, he invested ¥10 million ($90,000) in a stock fund operated by a former elite METI official. Murakami Yoshiaki was 46 when he left the ministry in 1999 to open M&A Consultants (commonly known as the Murakami Fund). One of his main backers was a close friend Miyauchi Yoshihiko, the chairman of Orix Financial Services, a major leasing company.

Murakami also approached Fukui and six other Fujitsu staff to purchase shares in the asset management firm. By 2002, the fund was said to manage $470 million in assets, enough to buy large share-holdings of listed companies for corporate takeover. Murakami was popularly known as an aggressive and successful entrepreneur in the same style as Livedoor's Horie Takafumi, but his relationship with Horie brought about his downfall.

On 15 September 2004, Murakami met with Horie and recom-mended shares in Nippon Broadcasting System (NBS) as a very good buy. On 1 October, M&A purchased 18 per cent of the radio network system. On 8 November, Murakami met again with Horie, who dis-cussed plans to buy 35 per cent of NBS thus enabling Livedoor to join forces with M&A to take over the company. Murakami proceeded to buy 1.93 million additional shares in Nippon from 9 November 2004 through to 26 January 2005 for ¥9.95 billion, and then sold approxi-mately 5 million shares in February when Livedoor bought a large number of shares in a takeover bid for Nippon, which was initially foiled by Fuji Television, a company that was connected to NBS through joint shareholdings. The Murakami Fund reaped profits of ¥3 billion while Murakami personally earned ¥150 million from the transaction.

When Murakami was arrested on 5 June 2006 on charges of insider trading, a further investigation by public prosecutors revealed that Fukui had not sold his shares in the fund when he assumed the post of governor of the BOJ in March 2003 (there is no law that prevents former BOJ staff from resuming employment in the BOJ). Although Fukui disclosed personal assets and stocks internally, there is no law that stipulates that the BOJ Governor must publicly disclose his personal assets. Fukui had not transferred the shares to a third party nor had he put the shares in a trust, thus enabling him to sell the shares at leisure. On 21 June, admitting that his investment had earned ¥22.31 million in seven years (as of December 2005), Fukui apologized for what could be construed as a conflict of interests.

It was further revealed that two months before he assumed his post, Fukui had purchased 10,000 shares in Mitsui O.S.K. Lines; 5000 shares in Kikkoman Corp.; 5000 shares in Mitsui Fudosan Co.; 5000 in Fujitsu Ltd.; and 10,000 shares in Nippon Steel Corp. The market value of the total shares was ¥13.31 million in January 2003, two months before Fukui became governor. At the end of May 2006, the shares were worth ¥34.76 million.[7] It was also disclosed that Fukui had served as an outside director at Mitsui O.S.K. Lines Ltd, Fujitsu Ltd. and Kikkoman Corp.[8]

According to a public opinion poll taken by the *Asahi News* a few days after Fukui's apologies, 62 per cent of Japanese polled wanted Fukui's resignation, even though he had not violated any law. Nevertheless, Koizumi supported Fukui's continuation as governor. Fukui pledged to liquidate all of his shares and donate the profits to charity. He also promised to retain only six months of his annual salary.

The bureaucracy and big business: the Ministry of Defence and trading companies

A scandal revealed in October 2007, involving the re-established Ministry of Defence and trading companies, is a fitting example of the staunch relationship between the ministries, big-business and politicians. It also draws attention to the ministry's procurement regulations.

Japanese trading companies are in METI's administrative jurisdiction and play a major role in the procurement of defence-related equipment from foreign manufacturers because the ministries are prohibited by law to purchase equipment directly from the suppliers. The trading companies facilitate such items as contracts and customs procedures for foreign manufacturers. They also collect information for the Japanese government that identifies the defence products that are scheduled to go on the market during the next five to ten years.

Although Japanese manufacturers of heavy industries (also in METI's administrative jurisdiction), among them Mitsubishi and Kawasaki, produce weapons for domestic use, they are forbidden by law to export. Therefore, they cannot compete with foreign manufacturers who produce under licensing agreements in Japan. As a consequence, military hardware purchases can be ten-times more than in the United States and European countries.

About 100 trading companies are registered with the Ministry of Defence and they are fiercely competitive about being designated as the sole agent who can monopolize procurement of parts from overseas and for contracts: 7 per cent of the ¥2 trillion annual budget for procurement of equipment by Japan's Self-Defence Force is spent on imported components and other parts that are handled by trading companies. In fiscal 2005, the total contract amount for imports was ¥152.5 billion.[9] Over 70 per cent of the contracts awarded are no-bid contracts.[10]

In October 2007 former Vice-Defence Minister Moriya Takemasa admitted in the House of Councillors to breaking ministry regulations when he and his wife had accepted invitations to play golf with the president of a company that had business dealing with the ministry while he was the top bureaucrat at the ministry. Regulations forbid Defence Ministry officials and members of the Self-Defence Force from playing golf with employees of companies that conduct business with the ministry. Moriya has accepted 12 golfing trips (¥3.89 million) and 108 one-day golf excursions (¥4.97 million).[11]

Moriya had resigned from the ministry in August over a disagreement with the Cabinet Defence Minister Koike Yuriko over his successor. Moriya was known to keep detailed notes regarding whom he met and the subjects discussed. When he resigned from the ministry in August, he burned all of his records, claiming that he was angry with Koike who wanted him retired.[12]

Moriya and his wife were arrested a month later for accepting the bribes, which are predicted to exceed ¥10 million, between 2003 and 2006.[13]

Moriya joined the Defence Agency in 1971 as a career official on the fast track. He was appointed administrative vice-minister of the agency in August 2003 and played a fundamental role in the upgrading of the agency to the Ministry of Defence.

Moriya had often played golf with Miyazaki Motonobu, the former senior managing director of Yamada Corp., whose trading company's ¥34 billion in sales included ¥9.436 billion in contracts with the ministry. Yamada Corp. was the sole agent for General Electric Engines and procured the planned transport aircraft the CX from GE engines for the Self Defence Forces.[14] Moriya, who was known as 'the emperor' because of his powerful position, had urged the Defence Ministry officials to purchase the G.E. engines.

According to Miyazaki, Moriya had been a long-time friend. Further testimony given by Moriya to the House of Councillors Committee on Foreign Affairs and Defence, and by Moriya to prosecutors in Tokyo District Court following his arrest for embezzlement, clearly showed that Miyazaki had entertained Moriya and his wife often, had given Mrs Moriya gifts when Moriya was the head of the aircraft section at the former defence agency, and that the section handled parts that Yamada sold to the agency. When he was the director of the agency's secretariat in 2000, Moriya opened two bank accounts under the names of two retired officials. He asked Miyazaki to deposit ¥500,000 into each account. The money was transferred from a Yamada Corp. bank account in Japan.[15] He also allegedly received ¥300,000 from Miyazaki as a congratulatory gift upon his promotion. Moriya was arrested a second time in November 2007 for allegedly taking ¥2.18 million in cash gifts in May and June 2004 and ¥1.45 million in February 2006, using the funds to pay off family debts.[16]

Miyazaki, who was in charge of business transactions for a considerable period of time, was not only wooing Moriya but also two other senior politicians in the LDP. Moriya's testimony revealed that Miyazaki had entertained Kyuma Fumio, former defence minister in Abe's Cabinet and Nukaga Fukushiro, who is currently the minister of finance in Fukuda's Cabinet.[17]

After disagreements with Yamada Corps' owner over the control of management, Miyazaki exited the company and established a new company, Nihon Mirise Corp. in 2006. But not before he had established a slush fund held in a number of bank accounts and managed by Yamada's US subsidiary, Yamada International Corp.

Yamada paid ¥100 million ($900,000) to a group linked to Akiyama Naoki, former president of the US subsidiary, who was arrested with Miyazaki for embezzlement. Akiyama is the executive director of the Japan-US Center for Peace and Cultural Exchange, a Foreign Ministry-linked organization that was established in 1968. The members of the centre are American and Japanese politicians who lobby for defence industries and are experts in national security issues. Miyazaki had headed the organization until 2006. Kyuma serves as one of the directors of the centre. Yamada also allegedly gave ¥30 million to the centre in 2006.[18]

The former Defence Agency had commissioned the centre to conduct research regarding a project to remove poison gas shells in Fukuoka Prefecture that had been left after the war. The contract for the removal was awarded to Kobe Steel after bidding.[19]

Miyazaki used the slush fund to entertain top US officials in an attempt to gain entry into the US military, including its realignment in Japan. In May 2006, through his new company, he continued to entertain US officials in the State Department and the Pentagon in an attempt to procure business dealings that came from the realignment of US forces in Japan, which had reached a final agreement in May 2006. Miyazaki's company stood to earn ¥10 billion in profits for contracts on US military bases.[20]

Nihon Mirise Corp. was also competing with Yamada for contracts to act as agents for American firms such as Northrop Grumman and General Electric. Indeed, it was revealed that Yamada had planned to bribe two senior US government officials to act on behalf of Yamada, which imported parts used in the Air Self-Defence Force's E-2C surveillance aircraft produced by Northrop.

Both Moriya and Miyazaki were arrested again in January 2008 on charges of bribery. Moriya was also charged with perjury.[21] At his trial at Tokyo District Court the following April, Moriya pleaded guilty to charges that he had accepted a total of ¥12.49 ($120,264) from two Yamada officials from 2003–07.[22]

The bureaucracy and bid-rigging

The bid-rigging scandal involving high-ranking officials in the now-defunct Ministry of Construction (renamed the Ministry of Land, Infrastructure and Transport in 2001) that was described in Chapter 1 indicates that collusion between business and the bureaucracy occurs regularly and it can be argued that it has become an integral part of the administrative system. A national public service law was put into effect in 2000 and accepting bribes and interfering in the fairness of public auction or bidding is now a criminal offence with prison sentences of up to two years or fines up to ¥2.5 million. But businessmen and bureaucrats appear not to be deterred by the repercussions.

Bid-rigging scandals have become monthly fodder for the Japanese press as the two following examples illustrate.

In March 2008, the Japanese press reported that Takamatsu Masahiko, a senior career official from the Ministry of Land Infrastructure, had been arrested for accepting bribes from Makine Kazuya, president of a construction firm based in Nara Prefecture, in return for informing

Makine of the price of a disaster prevention project in a national park before public bidding commenced in the summer of 2005 when Takamatsu was the head of the ministry's office at the park.[23]

In April 2008, the Japanese press reported that Kurashige Yuichi, an advisor to a subsidiary of a Tokyo-based construction company, Penta-Ocean Construction, was arrested for giving bribes totalling ¥500,000 to Oshima Hiroshi, a senior career official in the Ministry of Education, Culture, Sports and Technology, who was arrested for a second time. Oshima, who formerly served as the director of the Department of Facilities Planning and Administration which directs the planning of infrastructure development in educational institutions, is only the second high-ranking official to be arrested since 1989.[24] Oshima was not the only official implicated in the bid-rigging scandal. Other top officials and retired officials of the same department were also entertained by Kurashige, whose company won eight contracts for a total of ¥3.09 billion, while the parent company Penta Builders won four contracts worth ¥370 million.[25]

The bureaucracy and big-business: METI's network with retailers and manufacturers

Public corporations in Japan can connect the ministries with big business as was previously illustrated by the case of the Japan Highway Corporation. Another example is the government-funded Industrial Revitalization Corporation of Japan (IRCJ) which was established on 16 April 2003 as a fully-owned subsidiary of the Deposit Insurance Corporation of Japan and entrusted with $80 billion to address the issue of non-performing loans. Corporate expansion in Japan during the bubble economy years of 1986–90 was funded by substantial loans from national and regional banks. Many of the loans were underwritten by the rising value of real estate. After the bubble burst and real estate values fell heavily, the banks were left with a large body of non-performing loans or 'bubble loans'. Non-performing loans are, as stated, loans that are not currently accruing interest or on which interest is not being paid.

Kobayashi Keiichiro contended in 2004 that during the 1990s, the banks simply denied the bad-loan problem and that the official declaration of non-performing loans in 2004 was ¥35 trillion.[26]

The official function of the IRCJ was to purchase loans from creditors and remove conflicts of interest between the main bank and other creditors. In this way, the rehabilitation of the borrowers could be facilitated. The IRCJ selected failing firms that were considered suitable for rehabilitation, acquired the liabilities of the firms, persuaded the banks to forgive a substantial amount of the debt, thus eliminating non-performing loans, selected a firm or firms deemed appropriate for sponsoring capital investment in the floundering firms, and, together with the sponsoring firm, implemented a restructuring programme. The IRCJ was given two years (until 31 March 2005) to accept applications from banks and their major clients and to approve assistance of the firms, and three subsequent years to dispose of all liabilities.

At its launch, the target number of firms to be helped was approximately 100. At the end of March 2005, however, when the period ended for receipt of applications for support, the IRCJ had accepted only 41 firms for rehabilitation. Initially, there were 130 employees in the IRCJ. The majority of these were seconded from the private sector to work in the IRCJ because it was assumed that one of the main functions was the restructuring of business plans and reinvigorating management. But within a year, almost half of the members had left because there were simply too few firms being considered by the IRCJ.

The main reason for the lack of deals was the reluctance of the banks to accept the IRCJ's assessment of the value of assets held as collateral. The IRCJ purchased loan assets from the creditor banks of the failing firm, but only after the creditors agreed to carry some of the losses by waiving loan claims that were considered in excess of the value of the collateral. The banks were concerned that if the IRCJ's assessment of the value of the collateral was less than their assessment, they might be forced to relinquish a greater portion of the loan claims and to open their books to public scrutiny. As was previously stated, until well into the 1990s the banks had been protected by BOJ and MOF officials who were on the regulatory agencies boards.[27]

One of the missions of the IRCJ was to introduce more rigorous and transparent financial analyses and accounting practices into failing firms such that they could then be restructured financially to become viable. By addressing the issues in a number of firms, it was hoped that the practices would then diffuse widely into other problem firms outside the immediate remit of the IRCJ.

The IRCJ was not tied to a single ministry, but the firms in the sectors being assisted by the IRCJ represented construction and transportation companies (in the administrative jurisdiction of the Ministry of Land Infrastructure, Transport) and manufacturing and retailing (METI). Two of the major firms chosen for restructuring were Daiei Inc. and Kanebo, both in METI's jurisdiction. The following two examples illustrate METI's guidance of the retailing industry and its relationship with the IRCJ. As importantly, the case of Daiei reflects the consequences of poor monitoring by MOF concerning how Daiei's main lenders dealt with requests from Daiei to continue loaning, even though it was burdened with debt. Shoda Masashi, an analyst at Nomura Securities, told *The New York Times* in 2002: 'Daiei's problems reflect the problems of the whole banking industry.'[28]

Daiei Inc.

Daiei Inc. is a giant supermarket chain store in Japan which was established by Nakauchi Isao in 1957 as a discount retailer. During the late 1970s, the company began opening stores in Asia, America and in Europe. In the 1980s, the company began to diversify into real estate, leasing, shopping centres and a baseball team. Even though the bursting of the bubble economy had significant effects on Daiei's profits, which, in part was due to the slowdown in consumer spending, the company continued to borrow heavily from banks.

When Daiei was accepted by the IRCJ for restructuring on 28 December 2004, its debt had totalled ¥1 trillion. Daiei's main lenders were UFJ Bank, Mizuho Corporate Bank and Sumitomo Mitsui Banking Corporation, who insisted that the company apply for assistance from the IRCJ. Daiei resisted seeking government intervention for months, but finally acceded to the banks' demands.

The tell-tale sign that Daiei's financial woes were being monitored by METI was the announcement on 7 December 2000 that the founder Nakauchi Isao was retiring as Chairman and that Amagai Jiro, a former METI official, would replace him.[29] Amagai resigned as the head of the Equity Bureau of the National Personnel Agency (the agency that officially administrates *amakudari*) to assume the post.

He had joined MITI in 1968 and was involved in the retail industry when he was in charge of implementing the Large-Scale Retail Stores Law.

Daiei's declining sales of over a decade were only partly due to the slowdown in consumer spending and over-diversification. It was also competing for supermarket dominance with Ito-Yokado (Seven-Eleven) and Aegon. In August 1998, in order to reduce interest bearing debts that were estimated at ¥2 trillion, Daiei began to divest itself of assets such as the Ala Moana Shopping Center in Honolulu, Hawaii, and to close stores. After Daiei predicted a ¥9.8 billion loss in August 1999, it sold 25 per cent of its 35 per cent shares in Recruit Co. to Recruit firms for ¥100 billion.

Despite efforts to stem losses, Daiei's fortunes continued to decline and in November 2000, it announced losses for the year at ¥240 billion and predicted an additional net loss of ¥130 billion. It also announced plans to restructure by closing 32 stores and laying-off 4000 staff. Simultaneously, Daiei asked Sumitomo Bank, Tokai Bank and Fuji Bank to buy ¥120 billion in new Daiei shares. The trade-off was that officers from the banks would replace some of Daiei's existing directors to aid with the restructuring.[30]

And even with the divestment of assets and the issuance of new shares, Daiei continued to sink further into debt. Marubeni Corp., the giant trading company that owned 25 per cent of Daiei shares, agreed to purchase 5 per cent more of the company's shares as well as an additional 10 per cent of Maretsu Inc., a supermarket chain that is a Daiei affiliate, bringing Marubeni's stake in Maretsu to 20 per cent.[31]

Nevertheless, Daiei's debts refused to disappear. On 20 March 2002, Daiei asked the government for aid under the Industrial Revitalization Law. Tax breaks would amount to ¥600 million. The firm also applied to METI for grant subsidies to the parent company. Daiei then asked its three main lenders, UFJ Bank, Sumitomo Mitsui Banking Corp. and Fuji Bank for ¥520 billion in loans.[32] The banks had no choice but to acquiesce because Daiei's potential default on loans could portend to losses of ¥2 trillion. The loans granted amounted to ¥400 billion and on 27 April METI granted Daiei preferential treatment so that the firm and its 109 companies could receive tax breaks and be eligible for loans at lower interest rates from the Development Bank of Japan (DBJ), a Special Corporation that is currently undergoing privatization.[33] In October 2002, the DBJ announced that it would invest ¥10 billion in Daiei.[34]

Daiei continued to pare down its operation by selling off its English pub chain subsidiary the following December and in January 2003, it sold four hotels to Goldman Sachs Group, Inc.

However, despite the aid from Marubeni, bail-outs from banks and from the government, the group continued to be plagued with interest-bearing debt and net losses. On 18 October 2003, the group announced that net profits plummeted 98.4 per cent to ¥2.3 billion during the first half of 2003. UFJ Bank (to which Daiei owed ¥400 billion), Mizuho and Sumitomo Mitsui began to pressure Daiei to seek assistance from the IRCJ, but Daiei refused and tried to raise capital from private sources. By wiping off Daiei's loans from its books, UFJ would be able to dispose of NPL by 50 per cent.[35]

The banks approached the IRCJ for help in August 2004 but Daiei, concerned that the IRCJ would pressure it to sell off its baseball club the Hawks to corporations proposed by the IRCJ, would not cooperate and tried to raise funds from the private sector. Although the IRCJ attempted to assess Daiei's assets in September, Daiei's management was uncooperative. But finally, Daiei's management agreed to join its main lenders and formally applied to the IRCJ for assistance in October 2004.

Takeover bids to the IRCJ by foreign firms such as Wal-Mart were rejected in favour of Marubeni, the giant trading company that had owned a stake in Daiei. Since METI's administrative jurisdiction includes trading companies, its territory remained in safe hands. In his article for the Council On Foreign Relations, Edward J. Lincoln wrote about the barriers to foreign acquisition in Japan, in spite of Koizumi's promises in 2005 to double foreign direct investment:

> In January, the government's Industrial Revitalization Corporation of Japan weeded out all of the foreign firms bidding to rehabilitate Daiei, narrowing the competition to only Japanese bidders. Worse, at the end of January the Ministry of Finance announced plans to dramatically increase capital gains taxes for foreigners profiting from the resale of firms they have acquired.[36]

Kanebo

In 2004, Kanebo, the textile, food and cosmetic conglomerate, was saddled with debts of ¥520 billion when Kao, Japan's leading manufacturer of toiletries and household and industrial cleaners, offered to take over the cosmetic division for ¥400 billion. But Kanebo refused the offer and asked its creditors to forgive ¥99.5 billion in loans. However, the banks refused and the conglomerate sought the help of the IRCJ, who purchased its core cosmetic division for ¥380 billion (£1.9 billion).

Kanebo's decision was not entirely in its best interests. In May 2005, the IRCJ charged the popular company with accounting fraud. Evidently, Kanebo had a negative worth for the previous nine years, but had disguised its financial troubles by altering the books. Furthermore, Price Waterhouse Coopers Aoyama, Kanebo's auditors, had cooperated in the effort. On 13 June 2005, the Tokyo Stock Exchange de-listed Kanebo, whose stocks had been publicly traded for 114 years. PWC Aoyama was sanctioned and suspended from auditing for two months.

In 2006, Kao, along with three private equity firms, won the bid for Kanebo's cosmetic division. They agreed to pay ¥425 billion ($3.66 billion), including a ¥146 billion debt, which it planned to refinance. The bids from foreign producers including Johnson & Johnson, P&G and L'Oreal were rejected, once again leaving METI's territory intact.

A primary mission of the IRCJ was to encourage more transparency in auditing practices. But the IRCJ's intention to address issues of financial analyses and accounting practices did not necessarily relate to the firms that were selected to sponsor the restructuring of the failing firms. Realistically, the IRCJ's choice of firms was linked to assisting the banks that were experiencing difficulty recovering loans from zombie companies.

So far, the efforts by Marubenei and Kao to restructure Daiei and Kanebo have been hampered by the accumulation of further debt and, consequently, they have themselves been burdened with more debt. Apparently, the IRCJ did not recognize the need to investigate Kao's corporate finances prior to making the decision to choose the company to restructure Kanebo. Kao was placed on negative Credit Watch by Standard & Poors in February 2004 after the company had announced its decision to purchase Kanebo.[37] The company had been in the black for seven years prior to the purchase, but in December 2005 Standard and Poors again issued a credit watch report that Kao's debt level had increased due to the refinancing of Kanebo's debt.[38]

The investigation into the accounting fraud at Kanebo also confirmed the interpersonal network between METI and the IRCJ following June 2005. Taizo Nakatomi Taizo, a high-ranking official and a former head of METI's policy planning office, had taken ¥29 million from a secret account that had been collected over a 30-year period from the Japan Keiren Association, a METI Special Corporation. The taxes from bicycle racing provides substantial revenue that ostensibly funds METI's Industrial Policy Research Institute.[39] METI Vice-Minister Sugiyama Hideji denied that there was insider trading and asserted that Nakatomi did not have access to special information. Although Nakatomi resigned from METI, he was not arrested for embezzlement.

In January 2008, Prime Minister Fukuda's private advisory panel proposed five major reforms of the central bureaucracy. In its report the panel proposed:

1. One agency to administrate and assess central government bureaucrats.
2. A Cabinet personnel agency which would decide on appointments of high-level bureaucrats. The agency would be headed by a state minister and would also promote the transfer of personnel beyond the ministries' territories.
3. Twenty-five per cent of bureaucrats would be hired annually and would ultimately bring mid-career hires from the private sector. This would half the number of career officers who would be eligible for promotion to high-level positions.
4. Contact between bureaucrats and politicians would be prohibited unless they served as Cabinet ministers, vice-ministers, parliamentary secretaries or political affairs specialists. They would be appointed by a ten-member state strategy, staffed from the national ministries, the private sector and academia.

It was anticipated that, as in the past, there would be stiff resistance from ministry officials and politicians.[40] And, indeed, the bill that was submitted to the Diet on 4 April was a diluted version of the panel's recommendations. The bill allowed the continuation of the ministries and agencies ability to manage the promotion of personnel, including fast-track career officers. The bill also permitted continued direct contact between ministry officials and politicians due to resistance from members of the coalition government, who contended that the ban would hinder discussion of various issues.

The passage of the bill was doubtful because of resistance from opposition parties, who contended that the bill avoided tackling one of the key problems in the civil service system, which was the ministries' control over the promotion of fast-track career officers.[41] However, Fukuda was determined that a bill would get through both Houses before the end of the Diet session on 15 June in order to regain the trust of voters, whose approval rating of his administration had dwindled to less than 20 per cent, partly because of a series of scandals involving civil servants. The LDP-New Komeito ruling coalition ultimately acquiesced to pressure from the DPJ and a revised version of the watered-down bill was passed which called for the establishment of a Cabinet personnel bureau to appoint high-ranking ministry officials, but which allowed the continuation of direct contact between politicians and bureaucrats. *Amakudari* was not addressed.

Part II
Inside the System

6
The Elite Bureaucracy: Prisoners of the System

> Who governs Japan is Japan's ruling elite bureaucracy. The bureaucracy drafts virtually all laws, ordinances, regulations and licenses that govern society. It also has extensive powers of 'administrative guidance' and is comparatively unrestrained in any way, both in theory and in practice by the judicial system.
>
> (Johnson, 1995)[1]

The events described in the previous chapter were the consequence of the interpersonal network between the bureaucracy and the private sector. While these relationships exist in all countries, in Japan the networks are engendered with such mechanisms as the ministries' public corporations and the *amakudari* system and further intensified by the continuous political support from the LDP and the reliance on ministerial guidance by the Japanese. Bureaucrats operate unsanctioned by law. They can be arrested for accepting bribes, as was the case for former vice-minister Moriya, but often they are allowed to remain in their agencies as long as they are loyal to their institution.

Although there have been bills drafted to curtail *amakudari*, the bills have so far failed to pass either House in the National Diet. Although attempts have been made to reform the ministries' public corporations through mergers, down-sizing, reduction of funds and name-changes, it appears that the ministries are still in control of the public corporations. And, in fact, retiring officials are becoming more dependent on jobs in public corporations and research institutes because opportunities for employment in the private sector are steadily decreasing.

The elite officials in the national ministries have traditionally been regarded as the elite in Japanese society because they have the authority to administrate the private sector and are considered more influential than presidents and CEOs of large corporations. But since the 1990s, college graduates have not been as enthusiastic about pursuing careers in the ministries.

In the past, university graduates may have opted to enter the ministries as career officers precisely because they could anticipate a lucrative post-retirement position in businesses or, at the very least, employment in public corporations. The work environment is comfortable and the responsibilities of their new positions are far less demanding than their former duties. The combination of their retirement benefits and income earned in their second career will provide them and their families a secure future.

It is also common for the progeny of civil servants, in both the national and local government agencies, to continue the tradition of working for the civil service. Also, applicants who graduate from the top universities with degrees in law and economics may not have the necessary connections in big business and hope that careers in government will culminate in a high position in a ministry and, consequently, yield future rewards for their families.

There are 18,000–20,000 career officers working in the Tokyo headquarters of the ministries. They enter the ministries after passing a difficult Level 1 entrance examination for the National Civil Service (with the exception of the Ministry of Foreign Affairs). Approximately 1000 candidates are considered for elite positions among these officers and the ministries vie for the most academically superior of the university graduates. After two gruelling interviews, 25 candidates are chosen by each ministry for grooming for elite careers. These officers are designated as suitable for all of the top positions in the ministries.

Tokyo University (*Todai*) is considered the most prestigious university for civil servants. Among the ministries that favour graduates from *Todai* for elite careers are the Ministry of Finance, the Ministry of Economy, Trade and Industry, and the Ministry of Land, Infrastructure and Transport. The majority of vice-ministers in these agencies have invariably graduated with degrees in law or economics from *Todai*. There is a concern among Japanese that the *Todai* clique creates insularity, and that officers who hold degrees other than law or economics or who have graduated from other universities can experience discrimination in terms of promotion. There are few among the latter who hold positions as directors of divisions and, generally, they are not sent to the prefectures to serve as the directors of local offices.

The non-career officers who are graduates of colleges and junior colleges or high schools sit the Levels II and III entrance exams. They normally serve as support staff for career officials.

The rigorous path of the elite

The institutional structure of private corporations and government agencies is hierarchical and promotion is based on the seniority system, making advancement slow. By the time a career official reaches 55, he can expect retirement within a few years to make way for a junior official. Since the 1990s, young bureaucrats have elected to leave the ministries because of the rigorous competition among elites for advancement and the early elimination process. Also, as was previously explained, post-retirement jobs in the private sector are decreasing.

The members of the classes of 25 are rotated every 2–3 years to new divisions and assessed on their abilities. There is an enormous pressure to meet the expectations of their new managers and their superiors. They come to understand that good standing among their superiors rather than the quality of their work is crucial to advancement up the ministerial pyramid. Factionalism in the ministries prevails and promotion is often predicated on the correct alignment with superiors who are members of the most influential faction. At the beginning of their careers, officers from the same class of 25 are all promoted at the same time but, gradually, during the next ten years, members are weeded out for promotion. Through a gradual elimination process, only a few members will succeed in climbing to the upper echelons of their ministries.

It is interesting to note that the resumes of most elite career officials do not indicate the responsibilities performed during the first 3–5 years in the ministries. One of the reasons is that during the initial period, which in the case of some agencies can be an extended boot-camp, the young recruits are carefully scrutinized on their ability as well as a willingness to adapt to a system that demands a total commitment.

The work is demanding and the hours are long. The officers, if they are single, will live in the ministries' dormitories. If they are married, they may live in drab, cramped government-owned facilities if they cannot afford separate housing. They do not receive overtime pay and secretarial support is random. Most officers do their own administration until they reach a relatively high rank. But the expectation of achieving influential positions in government provides them with the incentive to adapt to the tough environment. Despite the events during the past 15 years and a mid-career exodus from the ministries by some disillusioned officials, there is still a strong commitment among bureaucrats to their agencies.

Escape from the system: temporary relief from constant pressure from peers and superiors

The Ministry of Foreign Affairs officials are posted regularly overseas at embassies and consulates. However, officers in the other ministries, with the exception of the Ministry of Economy, Trade and Industry, do not have many opportunities to go abroad, other than for further education in a foreign university for 2–3 years during their early careers. For many, it is their first experience of living in different social systems and of having a respite from the constant pressures of the workplace. By and large, an education in foreign universities is intended to help officers interact with foreigners and to develop social skills to engage with foreigners on behalf of their ministries.

The United States remains Japan's security blanket, as its military protector in the Pacific and as its biggest consumer of Japanese exports. More elite officials have been sent to study at universities in the United States than at universities in any other country in the world. Universities have received large contributions from both Japanese government agencies and big businesses for establishing centres focusing on Japanese Studies, and officials are sent annually to such eminent institutions as Harvard, Princeton, Johns Hopkins and Yale. In the United Kingdom, elite officials are sent regularly to the University of Cambridge, Oxford University, the London School of Economics and the University of Edinburgh. But officers recognize that a degree from an illustrious American university acts to enhance a future career, especially for METI officials, because METI officials serve as Japan's chief representatives at trade negotiations. METI officials who are comfortable engaging with Americans and who have a network of friends in American government are invaluable to the ministry.

METI elite officers can be posted abroad three times during their careers, usually to embassies, consulates and branches of the Japanese Chamber of Commerce and Industry as commercial attaches or at overseas branches of the ministries Special Corporations. The Japan External Trade Organization (JETRO) operates 73 overseas offices, providing METI officials with ample opportunity to be posted abroad.

METI officials who are posted at JETRO overseas offices promote Japan's economic and trade policies to governments, businesses, the media and educators. The officials lobby governments on behalf of Japanese businesses, search for patents considered applicable to Japanese business interests and for small businesses with new technologies which are in need of capital investment for R&D. However, since the government is determined to cut public spending, the activities performed through JETRO could easily be consolidated at embassies, consulates and chambers of commerce without compromising Japanese industries' interests, thus reducing the number of the JETRO overseas offices. But METI would be reluctant to downsize JETRO because it is recognized by the government that the corporation has effectively become an extension of METI as the ministry's control over its industrial sector is shrinking. JETRO is indicative of how Japanese ministries can create work through their organizations that will expand budgets, provide post-retirement positions and connections with the private sector as well as administrative authority.[2]

A number of Japanese commentators have written critically about Special Corporations and *amakudari*, among them Tsutsumi Azusa, who was the former secretary-general for the Liaison-Council of Labour Unions in Public Corporations. In *The Monster Ministries and Amakudari: White Paper on Corruption* (*Kyodai Shocho Amakudari Fuhai Hakusho*),[3] he wrote a detailed account of the ministries' corporations and a chronological chart indicating the migration of retired MITI officials to Special Corporations (including JETRO overseas offices) who then moved on to upper-management positions in private industry or other Special Corporations.[4] Through the observation of JETRO New York, one of the largest JETRO overseas offices, the author can support Tsutsumi's views regarding how the ministries use their corporations.

It is generally acknowledged by the Japanese that since the 1980s, JETRO's functions as the primary publicly funded promoter of foreign direct investment in Japan and support mechanism for foreign businesses eager to enter Japanese markets have not served to increase FDI in Japan, and that the proliferation of offices around the world have been relevant only to the observation of Japanese business activities abroad and to keeping track of trade regulations, and foreign and domestic policies that can affect Japanese exports in those markets.

MITI opened JETRO's first American office in the late 1950s, registering it as a public corporation and not as an agency of a foreign government under the Foreign Agents Act of 1938. But the State Department sued the Japan Trade Council, an organization that had been established in Washington, DC, in 1958, for contributing 90 per cent of its funds to JETRO New York. Consequently, JETRO was obliged to re-register as a foreign agent.

The New York branch, and the largest office in the United States, is the base of operations for METI elite officials who commute to Washington, DC, to represent Japanese industry at trade negotiations and to lobby the interests of Japanese government and industry to US government officials.

Most of the JETRO staff is employed directly by the corporation, which is the case for all of the ministries' corporations. The elites who have been educated in the United States often are posted to JETRO branch offices in the United States because they speak sufficient English and because they already have US contacts. Naito was posted to JETRO New York in the 1980s and made many friends in Washington, DC, when he participated in the semi-conductor negotiations with the United States Trade Representative (USTR).

The asset-inflated economy spurs expansion abroad

The expanding Japanese economy during the 1980s prompted large-scale corporate investment abroad. Japanese mega-banks opened corporate offices in major cities in the United States and Europe and some regional banks followed suit.[5] Japanese small businesses, primarily in the service sector, also opened subsidiaries abroad to supply the larger Japanese companies that had operations in those countries.

Local governments and industrial organizations also sent representatives abroad to promote the products of industries and local businesses, using JETRO branches as bases for their activities. Since JETRO USA is registered with the US State Department, it is able to host various agencies and organizations that are not registered.

The offices are managed by JETRO staff posted from Japan for three years, but METI elite officials manage operational budgets. JETRO staff care for the needs of all representatives, including facilitating visas for the agents, applying for social security, health insurance, and procuring local staff to assist the officials with research and administration. The officers from JETRO Japan engage in public relations and promote JETRO as an organization that assists American small businesses to enter the Japanese market and do business in Japan and organizes seminars.

All of the officers, including METI officials, who are on loan to both JETRO's domestic offices and JETRO's overseas branches are regarded as JETRO staff, although they work principally as representatives of their agencies in one-man offices. As an example, an officer posted by the Kyoto Prefecture government will identify himself first as a member of JETRO staff. A representative from the Japan Highway Corporation would be considered a member of JETRO staff. Although the other public corporations and prefecture governments pay JETRO substantial fees for office space and support (which help JETRO pay the rent and justify its budget), the officers are expected to cooperate with METI in research projects and promotional events that are not related to their responsibilities for their agencies. They try to maintain a modicum of independence and to avoid duties connected with METI's objectives, but often they are pressured to participate, deferring to elite officials.

The posting of representatives overseas in public corporations may not be based entirely on merit. As is the case for other postings abroad in the ministries' corporations, often civil servants from both prefecture governments and the national ministries, who have displayed loyalty through their work, are sent abroad by their superiors, or, perhaps, they may be sent because a family member is an elite officer in the organization. But officers may also be chosen for duty abroad because their behaviour is considered outside the norm and disruptive to the workplace. The officers could be suffering from a mental disorder or, in some instances, alcoholism, and a posting overseas will isolate them from their colleagues.

In general, the officers attend their duties to the best of their ability, but their workload is far less strenuous compared to their responsibilities in Japan and they enjoy a 2–3 year hiatus from the pressure of the home office. Most of the officers' previous careers are not related to their current work and they receive little training before leaving Japan. The requests from their home offices to conduct market research, investigate trade regulations, laws, current government policies, environmental issues and industrial standards are usually forwarded to consulting companies who are on lucrative contracts. Other duties include guiding delegations of Japanese businessmen on tours of their regions, arranging meetings with businessmen and government officials for their organizations' officials and entertaining Japanese government officials.

It was observed that despite the relaxed schedule at JETRO New York, the hierarchical structure of Japan's governing system, with the national ministries on top and prefecture government towards the bottom, was well-defined, as is the case in the majority of Japanese government overseas offices. It was observed that there was no palpable difference in the etiquette displayed among civil servants, even though they are separated by thousands of miles from their peers and superiors. There was little integration between elite MITI officials and the other officers. Indeed, the four MITI non-career officers who were also posted at JETRO New York normally did not socialize with their superiors. Ministry elite officers also tended to remain aloof from the local government officials unless there was business to discuss. All staff displayed a marked deference to MITI elite officers and the Japanese businessmen who frequented the office also displayed deference to MITI officials. The constant contact between JETRO and Japanese and American businesses gave the officers the occasion to establish a relationship with these firms.

The majority of the officers expressed little concern about either Japan's recession or the need for structural reforms in their administrative system. *Amakudari, shukko* or *yokosuberi* were never mentioned as these were an integral part of the civil service system and overseas postings were some of the rewards offered by that system. Interestingly, like most Japanese, they were remarkably passive about their political system, preferring to defer decision-making to their elite superiors. However, there was an implicit understanding that deference to elite officials was essential to one's survival within the system.

A number of the officials posted at JETRO New York had never lived abroad and their comprehension of English was superficial. The complex Japanese language is rarely spoken outside of Japan and some of the officers felt at a distinct disadvantage and on the defensive because they could not easily communicate with Americans. Furthermore, all of them had worked as members of divisions and had never worked independently, which, for some officers, was stressful. They were entirely dependent on JETRO managers for settling in New York and the officers did not tend to stray far from the office. JETRO management exacerbated a latent xenophobia among the officers by releasing news bulletins about crimes perpetrated against Japanese tourists throughout the United States. The officers were continually cautioned about racism, drugs and the proliferation of gun-related incidents in the United States. Consequently, the officers were always anxious about living in a country where they could be the victims of violent crime.

Escape from their system

For the majority of the officials, a posting in the United States is an opportunity afforded to a minority of Japanese civil servants, a rare and luxurious experience. Similar to government representatives and corporate executives who are sent abroad from other countries, the Japanese officers who are married are relocated with their families and they enjoy a standard of living that they would never experience in Japan. Homes are spacious, often with gardens, a phenomenon in Japan where land is at a premium, especially in the metropolitan areas. The officers also receive an allowance for their children's educational needs.

Ironically, despite their concerns about safety in the United States, and, in some cases, ambiguous attitudes regarding US–Japan relations and American mores, they recognized that America offered a physically easier and mentally calmer life-style than the Japanese civil service, and some Japanese officials can use their stay at JETRO New York as a means of escaping from their system. At the time of observation, the majority of elite officers seemed satisfied with their status, knowing that upon their return to their ministries they would receive a promotion. However, some of the other officers were desperate to leave Japan. JETRO staff, prefecture government representatives and representatives from other agencies, coveted work permits ('green cards') in order to gain residency in the United States. Since children who are born in the United States are granted American citizenship, their parents can live in the United States as their children's guardians. Therefore, it was popular among the officers and their wives to bear children during their stay.

Perspectives about America from inside the system

It was stated that the officers posted at JETRO branch offices in the United States are responsible for researching America's markets for Japanese business ventures, the macro- and microeconomy, and the political issues that would affect US–Japan trade relations. Also, consulting firms were contracted to do much of the research. But ultimately, the officers' analysis of these reports, and of the data they collect and send to their home offices, is affected by the officials' perspectives of the United States, which are based on their education about America and their exposure to American society.

A number of officials posted at JETRO New York in 1994 graciously allowed the author to interview them about their education and their impressions of the United States. They were relaxed because they were on extended leave and thus seemed freer to communicate candidly about their attitudes towards the United States. Also, the efforts by ex-LDP politicians to reform the political system in 1993–96 evoked a more liberal and, therefore, easier environment.

The excerpts of the interviews in the following chapter are taken from the interviews conducted with three METI career elite officers, a METI non-career officer, a JETRO officer, an officer representing a prefecture government and a vice-president of the North American Bureau of a major trading company, whom the author met at JETRO since Japanese business leaders congregated monthly at JETRO New York for meetings with JETRO and METI officials.

The questions posed regarded their initial exposure as children to the United States, their primary and secondary education about the United States and their initial contact with foreigners. The questions included the ease of access of information concerning the United States, their views on Japan–US economic relations and Japan's status in the global political economy. The officers were not asked personal questions but openly expressed their views regarding American society, views that are commonly shared by other societies as well.

Elite ministry officials are posted overseas because they are considered loyal to their ministries and will portray Japan's political economic objectives positively to foreigners. They are coached extensively on the proper etiquette in dealing with both Japanese and foreigners who are not connected with their ministries. For this reason, questions that would be considered politically sensitive were not posed.

7
The Interviews

A. METI elite career officer

The METI elite officer was a graduate of Tokyo University with a law degree. He was politically conservative. His views about America and American society were generally positive. In his early forties, he had a penchant for hunting and fishing and country music. When he returned to METI, he assumed the position of Director of the Imports Division.[1]

B. METI elite career officer

The officer was regarded as an 'atypical bureaucrat' because of his liberal perspectives, which could be one of the reasons why he was not promoted to vice-minister. Another, and perhaps more pragmatic, reason was that he was not a member of the OB *Todai* clique within the ministry because he had graduated from Kyoto University, albeit with a degree in law. The official's career path illustrates that promotion within the ministerial system can often hinge on an official's political ties within the organization and his relationship with his superiors.

He had been posted abroad three times before arriving in New York, the first time at a Japanese embassy as First Secretary. He was sent abroad a second time to an American university for a short period to study management, and then for one year as a research fellow in London. He was posted to JETRO New York for two years.[2] After returning to METI where he worked for two years more years, he migrated to another Special Corporation where he bided his time before migrating to yet another Special Corporation where his career ended. During his time at JETRO New York, the officer innovatively represented his ministries interests, especially the promotion of industrial policies and trade policies to American academia and to American government officials. He was 46 years old.

C. METI elite career officer

The official graduated with a law degree from Tokyo University. His father was in the Coastguard and did not have contacts in business; therefore, the official opted for a career in the civil service. He was sent to John Hopkins University in 1982 for one year of study. His analytical skills helped him to produce a high standard of work while he was posted at JETRO for three years. He was 40 years old.

D. METI non-career officer

Non-career officers can be posted abroad if they have expertise in certain fields, such as engineering. This officer had intended to train as a pilot at the Air Force Academy and enter the Air Force. However, after the war, all military institutions had been closed down; therefore, he decided to earn a degree in aeronautical engineering. He entered a major automobile manufacturer as a designer because the defence industry was non-existent and the civilian aircraft industry was very limited. According to the officer, many people with degrees in aeronautical engineering entered the automobile industry. He took full advantage of his stay in the United States by travelling to all of the 50 states during his three years tour of duty. He was 36 years old.

E. JETRO officer

The officer received a degree in economics from Keio University. When he was 31, JETRO sent him to the Wharton School at the University of Pennsylvania for two years where he earned a second degree. His father was a vice-president of a major chemical company. He married a Japanese woman while he was posted at JETRO New York and they had two children in the United States. After his return from JETRO New York, the officer left the corporation to study and live in the United States. Despite his initial concerns about racial discrimination in America, the officer settled his family in the southern United States. He was 40 years old.

F. Officer of prefecture representative office

The officer was not a native of the prefecture where he worked and he often spoke about the problems he experienced trying to integrate into the workplace of a prefecture that is well known among the Japanese for being closed to people who are born outside of the prefecture. He confessed that due to the stress, he had gained 20 pounds since entering the prefecture government and suffered from depression. It could be suggested that the officer was sent to JETRO New York because his colleagues considered him an outsider with mental issues. He had difficulty coping with his work at JETRO because he had not been sufficiently prepared before his posting. Regardless, he was extremely intelligent, one of the most liberal officers at JETRO and he would have been a successful promoter of his prefectures local businesses if he had been given direction. He was 39.[3]

G. Vice-president of a large Japanese trading firm

The executive had previously been posted at the company's branch office in the mid-west. He had lived in the United States for ten years altogether and had substantial exposure to America political society. He was representative of Japanese in upper management who are posted abroad a number of times. He was 50 years old.

Impressions of America during childhood

Although the men were not born during the war, their childhood impressions of the United States were connected to Japan's defeat and the American Occupation Forces in Japan. They had heard from their parents about the poverty and suffering of the Japanese and the aid received from the United States. During the late 1940s and 1950s, the Japanese regarded the United States with both awe and trepidation. Everything American was on a much larger scale, even the stature of the American soldiers. They were acutely aware of the discrepancy in the luxurious living standards of the soldiers and the poverty of the Japanese. Although there was a sense of yearning for personal wealth and individual freedom, which was reflected in the movies produced by the US government to promote the American Dream and democracy, there was also an ambiguity in the way Japanese perceived themselves as a nation that had been defeated for the first time in its history. They felt inferior to Americans, as the following interview data from interviewees A to G reveals:

A. 'When I was in elementary school I saw various programmes about America on television. America looked like a very luxurious country with beautiful scenery. I saw the life of cowboys who looked dignified and yet arrogant.'

B. 'The Japanese saw America as the ideal country. Japan was supported by a large amount of American aid. Men from the Occupation Forces were in the town where I was living so I saw American troops often. The men had splendid physics. I thought that the bases were very luxurious. My main impression was the gap between the poverty of Japan and the abundance. I didn't see resistance to the Occupation but the Japanese who were attending elementary school, who were of a slightly older generation than I, felt great sadness at the loss of Japanese traditional values. Some authors like Mishima Yukio[4] and Ishihara Shintaru[5] saw the Occupation Forces as conquering devils and Japan as a pitiful nation. The Japanese, particularly at that time, were simply trying to survive so there was a strong feeling that America was supporting Japan. Social values completely changed. In a word (and this is true for the entire world), Americanization was taking place and, consequently, Japan was inside this giant wave.'

C. 'The impression of Japanese who experienced the war was that America was a big country. They also felt inferior to Americans. I learned that they had suffered from food shortages and that their lives were miserable. I did not hear much about the Occupation from my parents but I heard it from mass media when I was in elementary and junior high school. My parents didn't know about the war. My mother was a child during the war and had little knowledge other than that her father served in the military in Manchuria. The Second World War was a shocking issue for the Japanese. People could not explain the war or their feelings. My opinion is that as a nation and a people, we are not good at reflecting on or reviewing issues which occurred. We are not good at summarizing or examining

problems. This is why the transfer of information from generation to generation has not worked well. At least the occupation
was operated swiftly and directly. The Americans were very
clever because they tried to control the people directly by
using the Japanese government indirectly.'

D. 'Although I was born quite a while after the end of the Second
World War, the American Occupation Forces were still in Japan.
My first sense of America was that America defeated Japan in
the war. Until Japan's definitive defeat, Japan had never lost a
war. There was an army base in my neighbourhood. I was very
small so I don't remember seeing soldiers, but I saw many
American civilians who lived in my area. My impression was
that Americans were very large and that America was a powerful wealthy country. Americans lived very wealthy existences
with big cars and shopping centres. They were independent!
The Americans who lived in my town looked well-off and lived
in spacious quarters. On the other hand, Japanese lived in a
small area in over-crowded quarters.'

E. 'My father was in the Second World War. I didn't hear specific
things about the war, but I often heard about Japan's poverty
because of its loss of the war and how everybody suffered. Rice
and food were at a premium and it was wasteful to leave anything on one's plate. Subjects such as war dead, the peace pact
were not discussed much. Only after Japan became richer was
there talk about how Japan broke the peace. There was also
ambivalence about the US. The Japanese lost self-confidence
because of the loss of the war. Self-confidence was also lost
because everyone stopped telling their children about Japanese
culture, Japanese values and how they wanted their children
to live. My father kindly taught me various things, but he
didn't speak about Japanese culture, civilization or social values.
I think that this was true for most Japanese households.'

F. 'Since I was a child, my whole life I have thought of America
with yearning and admiration because at that time, over 30
years ago, Japan's economy was very poor and America was
overwhelmingly strong. When I was small, I was conscious to

a certain extent of the place called "America". There was more of a feeling for American than for Europe.'

G. 'My father joined the Japanese army during the Second World War and went to China. After the war, he took some kind of guardian job at the American Occupation Forces Headquarters in Washington Heights, Tokyo. My father was very rigid and spartan. So he really accepted defeat because the countries were quite different. The stupid thing about the war between Japan and the United States was that there was no competition. A loss of confidence was not true for my father. He was proud to be Japanese. I think that the Japanese who were younger than my father, who are now 55 to 65 lost confidence. Especially at the end of the war, they were of high school and college age. That generation lost confidence and that is why their children were not disciplined. They didn't want to teach their children Japanese traditions. That was primarily because of the loss of the war, the poverty and because America was wealthy.'

Education about America

During and directly after the Occupation, primary and secondary education included American history, geography and English. The illustrations in the textbooks depicted a vast and bountiful country populated by white Anglo-Saxons (WASPS):

B. 'The characters in my English readers in middle school were Jack and Betty, who were WASPs [White Anglo-Saxon Protestants].[6] I had the feeling that generally the United States was WASP. The image of the US was that everything was big. All of the adjectives used were exclamatory; "big" agricultural development, "large-scale" manufacturing, "big" investment. I thought that America was the greatest country in the world.'

C. 'Compared to other countries, my education about the United States was very good. Most of the information about daily life in the United States came from mass media, television or movies, and was fairly realistic. I had studied American history and the Civil War in high school and in college. Also many Japanese read "Uncle Tom's Cabin". It is a very famous book. I also studied about Affirmative Action[7] and knew that even though time had passed there was still discrimination against blacks. I remember feeling frightened walking down Fifth Avenue in New York because I had heard that there was racism there. But the education Americans receive about Japan is zero. It's crazy but sometimes it is less than zero!'

D. 'There was not much written about the United States in Japanese textbooks prior to the Second World War. The Japanese did not think that it was necessary to study about Americans, but if Japan had understood the importance of America during the war it would never have attacked it! The facts I learned about the United States in grade school were that America was 25 times larger than Japan and had twice the population. I learned the Roman alphabet by writing the phonetic pronunciation of Japanese words in Roman characters. I presumed that by learning the alphabet I would be able to read English. When I was in the sixth grade I went to the Tokyo Olympics. But I found that I couldn't read any of the English words written on the billboards or in the programmes. I thought that by just knowing the alphabet I would be able to read English. I couldn't get over how strange this was and I was a bit surprised. This was my first strong impression of things American.'

F. 'The textbooks in Japan do not really touch upon the Second World War. How it should be written before it is put into textbooks is the problem. Historians say that the war should be written about as it actually happened (like Japan's occupation of China), but the government says that Japan is not a terrible country, so there are conflicting views. There was nothing on foreign countries in textbooks during the war. If there was any information, it was probably erroneous. One takes this misinformation, these impressions with you when you go overseas. All schools teach English from middle school to college. English is considered the most important subject, but there are many mistakes in the education of English. It is taught almost daily with two classes; one for reading and one for composition. There are no classes given for aural comprehension or for conversation. Therefore, although Japanese spend many hours learning English, they can't speak. In Japan, English which is antiquated and stiff that Americans don't speak is taught, even in college. Practical English for people who want to work or study in America is not taught.'

Initial exposure to foreigners

With one exception, there were no foreigners attending the schools where the interviewees were educated, which is common in Japan. As is the case today, the majority of foreigners were working for foreign companies or governments for a three- to five-year tour of duty, and they were not inclined to learn the difficult Japanese language in order to communicate effectively. They sent their children to private American or French schools, where language and educational systems were familiar, rather than to Japanese public schools. Ex-pats preferred congregating among themselves instead of making the extra effort to associate with their neighbours, despite the language barrier.

The interviewees' first exposure to foreigners occurred either when they were students in university or when they travelled abroad. It is interesting to note that the officials equated students whose descendents were Chinese and Korean with being foreign.

B. 'There were no foreigners in my school - no Americans, Chinese or Koreans. I was a member of a pen-friends' club. I enthusiastically wrote in poor English to pen friends. The first person was a Taiwanese and then there was an Italian. I wrote to quite a few Americans but, in the end, there was little communication.'

C. 'There were no foreign students in my school, only Japanese. When I was in junior high school, I was travelling from Tokyo Station when a foreigner asked me something. I couldn't understand anything! I was shocked! It was shocking for me to meet someone who didn't speak Japanese. He was black. I guess if he was white, I would still be shocked! Three-years of English language study didn't work at all so I couldn't answer.'

D. 'There were many foreigners in my area and there was a small foreign complex. There was a boy in my school whose father was black and whose mother was Japanese. He had entered a Japanese school at kindergarten so he spoke only Japanese, not English. He was treated the same as the other Japanese students. Since the students were children, there was no racial discrimination. He was popular and had lots of friends because he was good at sports and a fast runner. He later transferred to an American junior high school. My first encounter with an American was when I was in college, during a trip to Kyoto at a youth hostel. He had a backpack and seemed very foreign, very American. He was about my age and tall. There are many races in the United States, but the same race has been in Japan since ancient times, although Chinese and Koreans immigrated to Japan a thousand years ago.'

F. 'I attended public schools and there were no American students. The Korean population in my district was 50 per cent. There were many Korean students from second and third-generation families. They had Korean surnames, but they spoke Japanese. I had many Korean friends. We were in the same class in grammar school, but there were some who transferred to schools for Koreans when they became older and I really missed them. They had become special childhood friends and I became lonely. Schools for Koreans only still exist.'

Introduction to American society

There was the strong impression that America was dominated by a white Anglo-Protestant population (WASP) which had been promoted not only by American television and movies, but also by American and Japanese news reports. The interviewees were keenly aware of racism and discrimination against blacks. They also considered that Americans would include Japanese as a coloured minority and were concerned that if they travelled to the United States they were at risk of being the victims of discrimination:

B. 'When I was a child there was no television, but movies were big and we received information through movies about other countries and cultures. There was a lot of yearning and admiration [for America], especially when I saw Disney movies. For the ordinary Japanese the abundant food and the luxurious way of life was a dream. General MacArthur wanted to transmit the good side of America to the Japanese so he banned the movie *Grapes of Wrath* for a long time. After I read the John Steinbeck novel and then saw the movie after its release in Japan, I realized that my yearning for America was biased.'

D. 'There was nothing written about WASPS in my textbooks, but the Japanese assume that America is WASP. Perhaps because of the war, we Japanese felt that Americans and WASPS were superior to us. But it seems that the control of American politics by WASPS is gradually changing because Americans are looking closer at Asia and the Pacific.'

E. 'There were no other nationalities at my school and when foreigners were spotted in town, fingers were pointed at them and "foreigner" was uttered because seeing a foreigner was unusual. This was probably more prevalent in the outlying areas. For Japanese, there is a kind of ambivalence because Japanese think that whites are superior because of their large stature and their eyes and nose are pronounced.

The first time I became aware of American society was when Robert Kennedy was assassinated in 1971 during his campaign against Nixon. When I was a child I thought that the population in the US was composed of three races: White, Black and Asian. I learned of racism in the US when I was in grammar school, because of the 1960 Olympics in Mexico; the winner of the 20 meter race, Tommy Smith, raised his fist to symbolize Black Power. There is a distinction made between blacks and whites, but the term "coloured" also makes the Japanese a subject of prejudice. The Japanese thought that the US was almost all white but, on the other hand, the assassination of Martin Luther King and then "Roots" [a television drama series depicting African-American history] made Japanese aware of blacks. Of course, we were conscious of discrimination against blacks and knew that it was dangerous, but we didn't really have detailed information. The Japanese were concerned and fearful of racial discrimination in the US and when I was around college age, I didn't know whether or not I could work in the US. I thought that I might have personal problems. I thought that I shouldn't go to America because of discrimination. The Hispanic culture is still too new. I still think that WASPS control the US and have most of the power. In 1962, the Apollo launch made a big impression on the Japanese. "The US is really ahead of Japan!"'

F. 'One impression which remains with me is that when I was six years old, President Kennedy was assassinated. That was when America was very powerful. It was shown on television a lot. I was very small so I don't remember the incident clearly, but I watched the television with my mother. My mother cried. I remember even now. No one knew anything about Oswald. The Japanese were afraid because this type of thing did not occur in Japan. When President Kennedy was assassinated news came out about blacks, school segregation, blacks being separated from whites while riding buses and individual rights. There was the image that America was a country that was centred on Caucasians. This is still the image today even though every year 100,000 people immigrate here. The number of people who are not white is changing greatly but, as always, WASPS occupy the top positions in politics and finance. Blacks and Asians can't get these positions.'

G. 'There is the children's song in Japan called "Blue-eyed Doll". This is a very typical Japanese impression of the United States. That's the impression I had as well. I didn't know any other colour but a white person. There was no black, no Asian, no Japanese American in my mind. WASP was the majority.'

American society/Japanese society

Despite significant exposure to the American political and business environment during their tour in the United States, the interviewees still considered that WASPS dominated the political economy. Some of them candidly expressed their concerns about racial discrimination of people who were other than white in the United States. It must be emphasized that other societies also have a similar apprehension. Only G admitted that foreigners who were not Caucasian suffered from racial discrimination in Japan. There was agreement that Americans were self-confident and tended to view the world according to their own values without regard to the values of other societies. In other words, Americans felt that the American way was the only way.

All of the interviewees observed that compared to Japan where prices of commodities, housing and food were expensive, the standard of living in the United States was far more luxurious and prices of goods were less expensive:

A. 'Japanese textbooks do not devote much space to America, but newspapers carry certain types of information. However, it is essential to see the real America in terms of the values that come from the different races settling here and are nurtured in a land of land. Within this land is a unity, a United States with individual freedom and a democracy. If Japan can understand America from this composition, then we [the Japanese] can discuss America's basic course and its destiny. We can understand America by knowing that its basic ideals and philosophies emanate from this ethnic diversity. Japan is a mono-culture and therefore, it is difficult for Japanese to comprehend. Japanese tourism has recently increased, but Japanese travel on set trips and they all see the same things. Many see America from this perspective but I don't think that the real America is written about, which is unfortunate. I think that people should go to a variety of places to study. This is where the substance lies.'

B. 'I first came to the United States in 1976 for six months and now I am here in New York City. Of course, seeing and thinking about various things, I feel that there are some aspects regarding the American Dream that are not justified. If I was describing what is America in one word, it would be "Puritan". Japan, like England is "Empiricist". The most pronounced difference between a Puritan country and an Empiricist country is that in a Puritan country there is definitely a sharp distinction between good and evil. Up until now, when I speak to Americans, more than 90 per cent of them think that the world is this way (Puritanism). Although this way of life does not rely on a god, there must be a belief in self and a confidence in self. A self-reliant country is an idealistic country. If there is no self-reliance and idealism, then a standard cannot be established. This standard is probably not clear in Japan. Beliefs and ideals are important but, basically, living and surviving in society is extremely important. Americans probably always have a point of reference, but actually, for one to live in a society there must be a lot of compromise. I am not entirely in favour of compromise, but living and surviving is absolutely not based on one's own one-sided beliefs and creeds. The individual should fundamentally have appropriate ideals and creeds and beliefs, and Americans seem to have the courage to look at the world through this simplistic perception. People from other societies can understand the universality of the American point of view, according to this way of thinking, in a clear and simplistic fashion. The way of thinking in Japan and in England promotes a unique double standard and possibly there can be some deviation. Furthermore (and I am not 100 per cent critical of America at all), over the long term a Puritan country demonstrates Puritanism to the point that friction will easily occur with other societies who have various social values.

I will give a timely example. There are now trade negotiations between the US and Japan. The latest pronouncement of US Trade Representative Kantor is that the reason for the continuing huge trade surplus is because of Japan's position as a nation. This problem, really in terms of numbers [quotas], clearly must be solved. But if you turn things around and look at it from Japan's perspective, the United States had a huge trade surplus up until 30 years ago. Americans worked very hard and made excellent products. The trade surplus was natural. If the Japanese wanted a trade surplus, they had to develop excellent products. When comparing how open the door is to Japanese markets and American markets, America's markets are far more open than Japan's. Compared to the present time, there are more American products in Japan than before because American products are excellent. When Americans during negotiations negotiate with the contention that Japan is devious, from our point of view, it is Puritanism. Big decisions based on one standard.'

C. 'Even among Americans there is not a common sense of values. There is the Judeo-Christian philosophy and individualism. I like American society and individualism. It's very important. A typical way of solving critical political problems or situations is to make things clear and transparent through an investigation by a committee that recommends improvements. I think that this is typically American. Most Japanese do not share these philosophies, although we do have a democracy. Although this may seem to be contradictory, I would prefer to see aspects of individualism not enter Japanese society in terms of pushing one's will too far, regardless of others. I am very ambivalent.'

D. 'Since coming to the US, I have realized how inexpensive food is here. America is a luxurious place. Food servings are very large. Americans leave food on their plates, which is wasteful. In Japan, at school we are taught at lunch not to leave any-thing on our plates. We are served small portions that enable us to eat everything and not throw anything away to conserve because we don't have natural resources. When I see left-over food, I wonder whether it is wealth or whether it is wasteful. Americans seem to like the big and the bountiful. The Japanese like delicacy and refinement.

In Japan, food and rent are expensive. Prices for all goods are very high so salaries don't go far. America is a land of plenty, with surplus, therefore, Americans do not feel that they must depend on government and can rely upon their own strengths and abilities to achieve success. Japan has an enormous middle class and there is a fair degree of depend-ence on government support. If the economy deteriorates, the people rely on government to enact measures to improve things. This practice is very strong. The Japanese middle class is larger than the middle class in the US, but their income is much smaller. There are certain aspects of Japanese culture that are superior to American culture, such as refinement and delicacy. But there is no individuality or inventiveness. The educational system may be responsible for this. The Japanese educational system is often referred to as "uniform" and "standardized". Students are raised to be equal and those who display individuality and superiority are suppressed. Students who are underachievers are pushed ahead. Students' opinions are suppressed because the teacher assumes that he is the one who has the knowledge.'

E. 'Until Japan's definitive defeat by the United States, Japan had never lost a war. During the Meiji Period, there was prosperity and other cultures entered Japan. Since America occupied Japan, we began to learn that American culture was superior to Japanese culture. The mind-set "America is wonderful! The West is great!" permeated the country. What was considered unique became integrated into mainstream Japan. Japanese ways were old and, therefore, in order to become prosperous, Japan had to modernize. Japan had lost the war and Americans had big physiques and were very tall. Japanese felt that they had to copy America and Japanese values gradually disappeared. Although there was nothing written about WASPS in my textbooks, Japanese assume that America is WASP. I felt some fear regarding America and WASPS. Perhaps because of the war, we Japanese felt that Americans and WASPS were superior to us. But it seems that the control of American politics by WASPs is gradually changing because Americans are looking closer at Asia and the Pacific.'

F. 'Rather than saying that my education about the United States was sufficient and that it prepared me for my stay here, I would say that what I thought America was when I was in Japan and what I found here was radically different. When I first came here, I didn't know many things regarding the American lifestyle and how to get along here. There is a different way of thinking. Even though I understood things intellectually, I really didn't understand and experienced many difficulties. It's been about two years now and there were times when I misunderstood or was misunderstood and suffered from these mistakes. It's good that I can be open about this now.

Basically, Americans and Japanese are different in various ways. The characters of the races are different. The basic underpinnings are different. Therefore, doing business with Americans can be difficult. Both countries should learn about each other's culture and way of thinking. I think it strange that Americans refer to their own base when viewing Japan and the Japanese refer to their own base when viewing America. In America, everybody is a different race. Things are said to be easy and smooth here, but when one actually comes here, one becomes half-afraid because one doesn't understand the language and Americans are large in stature. This is probably difficult for Americans to understand, but Japan is small.

In an American office one must have an objective and know clearly what one is doing. In Japan, it is not clearly defined so when I came here, I didn't know what I was supposed to do. Here, the pressure doubled because I was alone. In Japan, I didn't have to think and decide for myself, which is fairly usual. One doesn't act on one's own volition, but here one must decide and then report what you would like to do, and wait to hear the outcome. In Japan, a proposal is passed on to your superiors who consider it. There can be various problems with this because decisions are not made immediately. At the home-office, I worked together with many people so even if I didn't understand, I could ask other people. In a sense it's easier. However, all of a sudden I came here and I was alone. I have become used to it and I think that it has been a good experience.

I don't get around America too much because I work within a prescribed area. Experiences of racial discrimination happen only on occasion. When I went to Los Angeles, I was mistaken for a Chinese by a Caucasian and he told me to get out of America and go back to China. Many immigrants and refugees from China have immigrated to Los Angeles. WASPS and Caucasians are at the centre of American society, though. If companies were to employ a certain percentage of each race, there would not be that many Caucasian employees. There are many nationalities who are immigrating who don't speak English so in 50 years not only English but Spanish may also be a language of choice.'

G. 'What is America? Even if I tried, I wouldn't be able to explain what American social values are. Social values are different for each individual. In the US everyone is a different nationality, a different background. People who live in the same apartment building all have different values from their neighbours. This is America, I think. In Japan, everyone is the same. Japanese all have the same values. For Japanese earning a living and putting away a pay check comes first. Education comes next. Before the Meiji Period no one worked very hard. During the Edo Period there were only the *samurai*. Farmers really didn't work hard and merchants went drinking at night. Japanese started working from the Meiji Period or perhaps after the First World War. After the Second World War, they realized that they had to work hard to survive. It's still the case, but even if we don't work as hard as we used to, we will survive. The individual standard of living is good. Of course, there are people who think that they can improve their standard of living to higher levels. But I think that as long as there is rice to eat every day and money to meet daily expenses, it is fine as it is.

Such values as working for one's company, working for one's country have disappeared. The country has become wealthy. As for racial discrimination, I was told by Japanese people who were local staff for my company in San Francisco that there was much discrimination. But this was directly after the war in the 1950s. They had come to the United States as wives of American servicemen who had been stationed in Japan. They told me about incidents I have never experienced myself.

I had a Japanese friend who worked for the Bank of America in San Francisco. He came here when he was in elementary school so he was fluent in English. He felt that there was discrimination and that because he was Japanese, he would not be promoted beyond a certain point even if he performed well. Although it is said that in America, one is used for his ability, a Japanese working in an American corporation can't get ahead. I don't know if this was because, as an individual, my friend felt that he couldn't use his abilities as well as he would have liked or whether this was indeed discrimination.

This is also true in Japan with the use of employees. There is a bad kind of discrimination in Japan. As soon as a white person enters a Japanese company, they are treated with respect. They are set apart. However, people from neighbouring countries are treated badly. Japanese are devious. They don't mix with other cultures. Koreans, and now recently, Indians, Pakistanis, Bangladesh, Spanish can't enter Japanese society. It's terrible! Discrimination is discrimination. White people don't feel discrimination in Japan but among races like Filipinos, there are people who cannot find proper employment and gradually end up doing unsavoury and low-class work which Japanese won't do.'

Media coverage of Japan and the United States

The unanimous opinion among the interviewees was that since Japan depends upon the United States for its exports and for its security in the Pacific, the coverage of the United States by Japanese media is naturally extensive. There was also agreement that the coverage of Japan by American media is far less because Japan is not considered as important to the United States, but that there were many inaccuracies in the reports released by media in both countries, which led to misinterpretations regarding both societies. The views also pointed to concerns that while the Japanese must depend on America's markets, they are vulnerable because of it:

B. 'Before coming to the US, I knew pretty much everything about the American political economy and industry. I think that most Japanese do. Japanese papers report in detail on the United States. There's not much we don't know about. As for American mass-media coverage of Japan, America has more concern for global things like the Middle East and Saudi Arabia. It reports on everything concerning those areas. The coverage America gives Japan is not much.'

D. 'I don't know if it's a question of the US system of reporting news or whether Japanese mass media isn't doing a good job sending information to American media, but there is a big discrepancy between what is reported in the *New York Times* and the real facts. Japan is always subjected to criticism and accused of such things as industrial espionage and unfair trade practices. The reporting is very one-sided. However, in Japan the situation is the same. The Japanese press accuse American politicians of being dishonest and often report inaccurately. English-language newspapers like the *Japan Times* report news on the US but correct information is not often reported. I feel that it is unfortunate that there are many more articles on international affairs in American newspapers than there are in the Japanese press. Only on the international page in American newspapers are there sections on Japan. The Japanese press does cover in more detail South East Asia than the American press because of ASEAN, and trade between Japan and South East Asia has increased more than trade with the US.'

F. 'The United States is Japan's most important partner. Therefore, much of the news in Japan is devoted to the United States. However, when I came here, I found that there is not much about Japan in American newspapers. The Japanese think a great deal about the United States. However, as a trading partner, America gives the same degree of importance to European countries as it does to Japan. I feel that Japan is just one among them. There are many articles written about Japanese politics and economy in American newspapers but, in reality, articles on Japanese lifestyle and culture do not appear. There's plenty on business. I think that there must be more of an effort to promote Japan by Japanese at a grass roots level and by citizen groups, otherwise Japan won't progress and there will be no interaction on an international level. Japanese know America very well. They all know where America is located. But Americans don't know much about Japan. The whole world doesn't know much about Japan, for that matter!'

G. 'I hate mass media! The Japanese press does not transmit correct information about the US to Japanese. This should be of interest. Prime Minister Hosokawa came here a few months ago and stayed at the Waldorf Astoria. President Clinton also stayed there. There was very tight security. The heavy police protection was for Clinton, not for Hosokawa. This is not done to such an extent in Japan. The Japanese press reported that the police blocking off the street didn't give Hosokawa adequate security like they did to Clinton. The newspapers from other countries in attendance didn't complain. I wasn't there, but wherever President Clinton goes security is always tight and very disruptive. This unimportant news became fodder for criticism.

However, things that happen in Japan are very important. Everyone knew that Mr Kanazawa's [Kanazawa was a top official in the Ministry of Construction] acceptance of large bribes from the construction industry but no one wrote about it! Everyone writes about the Waldorf and Clinton! However, the *Washington Post* did write about the scandal.[8]

I don't feel that Japan and the US are equal. The interest and concern that Americans have for Japan and the interest and concern that the Japanese have for the US are completely different. Japan is not important to the United States. It's all right that ABC doesn't report news about Japan. But for Japan, America is very big. Trade with America is tremendous because the population in the US is tremendous and America takes huge amounts of imports. American's need for news about Japan is much less than Japan's need for news about the US.

In both countries inaccuracies in reporting are made on various economic facts from each country. There is the excuse that reporters want to report on things as fast as possible and, therefore, cannot get the complete facts. Because of this, I don't like to read the reports. I have not seen much news on Japanese culture here. This is the degree of importance which Japan has for the US. It matters very little. Even though Japan is the US's leading trading partner, America does it. There are car producers in America. Sony and Panasonic produce here. If American markets disappear, Japan could not exist. It would be a pitiful state. It is ludicrous to be angry about the degree of interest Japan has for the United States and the interest that the US has for Japan!'

Japan–US trade relations

All of the interviewees expressed disappointment that Americans' only interest in Japan concerned business and trade. Additionally, the United States' important trade partners included other countries besides Japan. Although they accepted the economic power wielded by the United States, they also expressed an explicit frustration with American's apparent disinterest in Japan, the second largest economy in the world. The general attitude among the interviewees, as well as the other officers posted at JETRO, was that Americans were wealthy and self-sufficient and could afford to open markets to Japanese products while the Japanese survived entirely on importing raw materials and exporting manufactured goods. It was clear that mercantilism would continue to be the foundation of Japan's future economic policies, despite huge trade surpluses and current account balances.

The perspectives also illustrated the Japanese' ingrained defensiveness when dealing with other competitive economies, namely South Korea and China, that loom as future economic and political powers in the global arena and surpassed the United States in 2008 as Japan's biggest trading partner. Inevitably, the Japanese must contend with a totally different set of issues, which include a turbulent history that is still a source of contention in Sino-Japan and Korea-Japan relations.

B. 'Wherever one goes in the world, English is understood, therefore Americans do not have the desire to learn about foreign countries. That's because America's bounty, American words and America's system supports the world. It's just the way things are, I guess. America is vast, the great supporter, America, the great provider, America. We are always aware of its presence. I think that the recognition of whatever relationship Japan has with the United States is within this context.'

D. 'Japan survives on trade. Japan doesn't have natural resources. If it doesn't import these resources, process them, manufacturer goods and export them, it cannot survive. The US doesn't depend on trade because it has natural resources and surplus. In order for the US Trade Delegation to negotiate effectively, they should be more literate about Japan's markets and consumer needs. They should speak Japanese. The official languages at the UN include English, Chinese, French, Russian and Spanish. Since Japan has become more important politically and economically than other countries like France, for example, Japanese should be adopted as an official language.'

E. 'Concerning America's request to Japan about the trade imbalance, America has so much that it only has to think of itself. The US is now looking at China instead of Japan because it is easier to enter the market. The Chinese language has more similarities to English than Japanese. Chinese resembles English in grammar and communication is easier between Chinese and Americans. Chinese resembles English because there are many phrases and sayings that are common in both languages. In Japanese, special terms must be invented in order to communicate. Also, Chinese and American preferences are more similar than Japanese and American preferences.'

Why can't the Japanese internationalize?

Despite the differences in ages and backgrounds, their views regarding the US–Japan relationship and Japan's position in the global political arena were remarkably similar. They reflected the general defensiveness felt among the Japanese that, although Japan is a big player in the global economy, Japan is the odd-man-out and at a disadvantage when engaging with the United States, as well as other foreign economic powers, because of its size, its insularity and the language barrier:

A. 'I don't think that Japan can internationalize. "Internationalization" is spoken about but, as I said previously, Japanese go abroad, have experiences but return to Japan and their same way of life. Unfortunately, things from the outside will never enter Japan smoothly. I really don't understand what "internationalization" is, but I think that for Japanese to achieve a level that enables them to negotiate and interact with various nationalities is difficult.'

F. 'Japan is a small island nation and insular. People are not open to outsiders. They build stone fences and close themselves off. Japan has internationalized in some areas like trade but for the general population, Japan has not internationalized at all.'

G. 'The rotating staff, even though they spend five years here, upon landing at Narita Airport, once they go through the doors at Narita, they forget everything they have experienced during the last five years. They must be real Japanese. That's the only way to live in Japan. The only way to live in Japan is to forget everything one has experienced. It is not only true in ordinary Japanese society, but it is also true in Japanese companies, even in this company still. No matter how many thousands of workers are sent to no matter how many countries, the Japanese will not develop an international point of view and will not become international. If one considers that the Japanese people live entirely on trade, Japan cannot afford to be isolated.

The Japanese who were sent here before me did not receive any education here. However, all of the Japanese who are posted here inevitably send their children to special Japanese preparatory schools (after regular school hours) as they do in Japan. They want their children to enter the Japanese education system. So even though Japan posts employees overseas for three to five years, Japan will not be able to internationalize. I don't think that the Japanese mind is too rigid, but the Japanese should try to understand world affairs. Being a tourist is no good. Japanese do argue that Americans who work in Japan for American companies leave without understanding anything about the society or culture. But Americans have a pretty good sense of themselves and the world because they go out into the world. You can't compare the two countries! Japanese go to other countries on a theme: on business, on an adventure, to the desert to feel the heat, walking around the world or living in the mountains. They sport a dishevelled look to fulfil a dream. But they must really ENTER those societies.'

In summary

The interviews were conducted when the Japanese government was releasing a series of stimulus packages to kick-start the economy. It was a brief period when politicians had absconded from the LDP to form several opposition parties in an attempt to implement political and administrative reforms. But there was no indication that the government fully recognized or were unwilling to confirm the extent of Japan's problems. Nor did the banks or corporate borrowers want to divulge the load of outstanding loans. There appeared to be a general denial among government officials that measures were needed urgently to carry forward initial reforms of the financial and administrative system.

The interviewees' responses reflected the extent to which Japan relied on the United States. The answers also revealed a distinct ambiguity regarding this relationship:

1. America was big, powerful, wealthy and self-sufficient.
2. America was Japan's protector in the Pacific.
3. America's markets were vital to Japan's survival.
4. America's only interest in Japan was business and was not concerned with Japan as a nation, even though it was the second largest economy in the world.
5. American politics and business was dominated by WASPS and could be biased in dealing with Japanese, whom Americans considered a coloured minority.
6. America and China had more in common than America and Japan in terms of consumer culture and similarities in language.
7. Japan survived entirely on the importation of raw materials and the exportation of manufactured goods.
8. Japan was the second largest economy in the world but received little recognition of this status by the United States.
9. Japan was the second largest economy in the world but not recognized by the United Nations in terms of making Japanese an official language (as was Chinese, French and Spanish) and of having a seat on the Security Council.
10. Japan was a small island nation and the Japanese tended to isolate themselves from other societies.
11. Japan would never integrate into the global political community.

These views are indicative of how Japan regards its current position in the global economic community. The Japanese are resigned to mercantile policies in order to survive, but they also feel vulnerable because of their dependence on the United States and now on China. The dependence on these two economic powers will intensify Japan's insecurity since its economy is extremely fragile. Furthermore, Japan's weakened economic environment together with its adherence to mercantile policies will determine how Japan reacts to the demands of other trading partners to open markets to imports, to foreign business ventures and to FDI.

Peter Mandelson, the European Union trade commissioner complained in a speech given at the EU–Japan Centre of Industrial Cooperation on 21 April 2008 that Japan was 'the most closed investment market in the developed world'. Ironically, the event was supported by METI and JETRO. Mandelson suggested that Japan, while taking advantage of the openness of foreign markets, was creating barriers to foreign investment. He cited figures showing that only 3 per cent of Europe's total €1900 billion ($3000 million) outward investment was invested in Japan, comparing it with the amount of Japan's outward investment. 'For every dollar Japan invested in the UK and the Netherlands alone, European companies were able to invest a net total of only three per cent in Japan.'

8
Conclusion

Too little too late: what ministerial policies have wrought

The conclusion of *Special Corporations and the Bureaucracy* (Carpenter, 2003) stated that even if the Japanese initiated structural reform of the administrative system, the reforms would come too late to bring Japan's economy back on track. That prediction still stands.

At the time of writing Prime Minister Fukuda's approval rating was 23 per cent, the lowest since he took office in September 2007, indicating that voters were discontented with policies in general, particularly with the new health-care insurance programme that requires premium payments to be deducted from pension benefits. Voters, who were paying more for petrol, were angry also about the bill that called for a hike in gas taxes that the LDP pushed through the Lower House at the end of April 2007. In May, despite the fact that some of the funds for road construction work in the past had been spent on leisure equipment and entertainment for officials from the Land Ministry and its affiliated public corporations, a bill was passed that limited the use of gas tax revenue for road construction during the next decade.[1]

When Abe's administration's approval rating plummeted to 26 per cent in the summer of 2007, the LDP suffered a humbling defeat at the poles, leading to Abe's resignation. It was predicted that Fukuda would also resign before the September general elections to make way for a younger ultra-conservative LDP politician. However, even if discontented voters give the DPJ more power in both houses in

2008, it cannot be assumed that policies will change significantly. *Special Corporations and the Bureaucracy* stated:

> Political bickering among members of the LDP and among members of the opposition parties has resulted in political gridlock. In fact, the philosophies of opposition parties that were once at opposite ends of the spectrum are now converging as the LDP platform encompasses their platforms. The Japanese are in political limbo.[2]

From the end of 2007, government began releasing monthly data that forecast a bleak year for Japan's economic growth. In December 2007, the government downgraded the GDP for 2007 to 1.3 per cent instead of the 2.1 per cent predicted earlier in the year. The Cabinet Office announced in February 2008 that consumer confidence in households with two or more occupants sank to its lowest level at 37.5 in January since June 2003 (36.7).[3,4] By May consumer confidence had declined to its lowest level since 2001 at 33.9 and was expected to deteriorate further. The Cabinet Office announced in April that the economic growth had 'paused',[5] reiterating that business confidence was weak due to fears of a recession in the United States and the steep increase in the prices of raw materials and petroleum.

Government debt to GDP ratio is the highest among the industrialized countries.[6] The debt will escalate further if the Bank of Japan normalizes short-term interest rates, which stand at 0.5 per cent, but this is still unlikely. The BOJ also predicted a much slower growth for 2008, based on mounting concerns about a recession due to the subprime crisis in the United States, and rising prices for material, commodities and oil.[7] In its biannual *World Economic Outlook* report released in April 2008, the International Monetary Fund (IMF) predicted that Japan's GDP in 2008 would not exceed 1.4 per cent in 2008 and 1.5 in 2009 due to the risk of a global recession and strongly recommended the BOJ to lower interest rates further.[8]

Japan's tight economic relationship with the United States was highlighted by reports that exports to the United States had declined during last quarter of 2007[9] and that the losses incurred by Japanese banks from the United States subprime mortgage market were far more than had previously been considered in 2007. The Financial Services Agency (FSA) announced in November 2007 that the subprime exposure for ten major banking groups, 110 regional banks and 445 cooperative financial institutions was ¥1.3 billion ($1 billion).[10] In February 2008, the losses were climbing to ¥600 billion ($5.6 billion) with Mizuho Financial Group Inc. and Mitsubishi UFJ Financial Group, Japan's largest lenders, suffering the largest losses at ¥490 billion ($4.57 billion).[11] However, in April Mizuho alone reckoned its losses to be ¥565 billion ($5.54 billion),[12] but by May the bank disclosed that total losses from the subprime loan loss was ¥645 billion ($6.1 billion) and that its earnings for fiscal 2007 fell almost 50 per cent to ¥311.22 billion ($3 billion).[13] The six major banking groups also conceded that their losses from the subprime crisis and the turbulence in financial markets for fiscal 2007 totalled ¥945.5 billion, 3.4 times the amount that was estimated in November. Profits dropped 33.9 per cent from the previous year.[14] Norinchukin Bank, Japan's second largest bank and effectively the central bank for agriculture, forestry and fisheries disclosed in May that subprime losses were reflected in a ¥186.9 billion loss.[15]

Although Japan has experienced six consecutive years of moderate growth, the economy has shrunk 9 per cent during the last decade. At the time of writing, unemployment had climbed from 3.8 per cent to 4 per cent and, according to data released by government at the end of April, wages in 2007 fell 1.7 percent from the previous year. Furthermore, since one-third of the labour force is non-regular employees the wage-gap is widening. It was stated in Chapter 1 that employment in SMEs account for 70 per cent of the workforce, but SMEs are either reducing capital investment or are in financial duress and their employees are suffering the consequences. The April 2008 economic survey released by the OECD stated:

> Increasing dualism in the labour market is closely linked to Japan's unbalanced recovery, both as a cause and a consequence.

The report also stated that the biggest problems confronting the Japanese were the expanding discrepancy between the wealthy and poor, the continuing deflation and mounting public debt.[16]

Japanese and foreign investment firms' outlook for 2008 was also gloomy. The general consensus was that the economy was likely to go into recession. The number of firms going public in 2007 on the Tokyo Stock Exchange had decreased 40 per cent from 2006 with 121 companies listing, which was 46 less than the previous year. New business start-ups were also slow because investor interest was weakened by the scandal involving Livedoor Co. and various other cases of accounting fraud in start-ups. Furthermore, the appreciation of the yen to ¥99 per dollar on 14 March 2008, the lowest in 12 years,[17] due to the weakening of the dollar, clearly showed that not only were Japanese manufacturers still reliant on exporting to American markets, but also that the bureaucracy's mercantile policies were no longer viable.

Microeconomic data released by the BOJ, METI and MOF revealed the significance of the problems that Japan was experiencing. The November 2007 Bank of Japan's quarterly survey of the business environment disclosed that 72 per cent of local business leaders did not feel that the country's economic conditions were improving. The general outlook was that conditions were deteriorating in most of the prefectures, which were plagued with mounting debt. Without a substantial injection of tax revenue from the corporate sector, they would continue to depend on hand-outs from central government. However, the BOJ's monthly report in June revealed profits were decreasing due to slowdown in exports and the rise in energy and material prices.

METI, the ministry responsible for planning regional economic policies, admitted at an emergency meeting in late December 2007 that its original assessment of sustainable economic growth had been overly optimistic, that business sentiment in ten regions was deteriorating substantially, and that due to rising oil prices and a plunge in housing start-ups, the support measures that had been planned months earlier for small businesses would be implemented by 31 March 2008. When it announced the following February the further deterioration of regional economies, METI again stressed the importance of the new loan programme for SMEs by a semi-state financial organization that will raise the lending capital to ¥48 billion from ¥20 billion without guarantees from third-parties.[18]

MOF released data in March 2008 indicating that overall capital spending fell 7.7 per cent, the biggest decline in five years.[19] In April, MOF downgraded the economy for the first time in six years and three months, declaring that it was at a 'standstill'. The announcement came after MOF's 11 regional offices reported a decrease in output and a deterioration of business sentiment in all regions during the first quarter.[20]

The Finance Ministry's budget for fiscal 2008 called for a ¥152.5 billion increase over the 2007 budget. The total budget of ¥83.061

trillion was the second largest annual budget. The supplementary budget suggested that Fukuda was grasping at LDP supporters among the aging population and in the rural areas who have traditionally relied on pork-barrel projects and subsidies. Special accounts are used liberally to top-up the supplementary budget for such items as the postponement of the aging population's burden of sharing more of the expense for medical care. And even though there have been further cuts in funding for public works (3.1 percent), ¥79.9 billion in direct subsidies will be allotted to rice farmers who are paid to substitute other crops for rice.[21]

A policy-guiding panel of the IMF in April 2008 strongly recommended that Japan push for further structural reforms in order to ward off the affects of a global economic down-turn and to stabilize economic growth. The IMF agreed with the BOJ that Japan's GDP in 2008 and 2009 would be 1.4 and 1.5 per cent respectively, which were 0.1 and 0.2 percentage points lower than had previously been predicted in January.[22] Also, due to the sharp rise in energy and food prices, households were cutting back overall spending.

At the root of the problem: institutional paralysis

Pressure from the IMF and the OECD to continue reforms will not propel the government to pick up the pace because it cannot. The Japanese are mired in a system of administration that is rooted in interpersonal relationships between an elite bureaucracy, a dominant political party and big business.

To complicate matters, the hierarchical structure of each ministry intensifies factionalism among the staff of the individual ministries, resulting in institutional insularity. And the on-going struggle among the ministries to maintain or to expand administrative territory and authority can paralyse the planning and implementation of policies.

The motivation for reforming the system must not be predicated on stopping the corrupt practices of a minority of bureaucrats and politicians that are a consequence of the system, but rather on the urgent need to restructure an antiquated model of administration, which is stalling the implementation of economic and social policies that can resolve the unremitting socio-economic problems that have been challenging the Japanese for years.

First and foremost, the overhaul of the system should commence with the reorganization of the civil service and the elimination of some of the ministries' public corporations and the abolishment of *amakudari*. However, alternative incentives must be provided in order to promote careers in government to talented college graduates who now would prefer to enter the private sector for more satisfying careers.

Officer C stated the general views of bureaucrats regarding the post-retirement system:

> The Japanese bureaucratic system is unique. Our management system is different from the typical Japanese corporate management system. We retire early. Official X entered MITI in 1965, so he retired. He worked for 25 years in MITI. Of course, he got a new job in another organization. I have already worked for 15 years and I'm sure that I'll work for ten more years, at least, but no more than 15 years.

Since the system has yet to be reformed, the officer, after his retirement, will probably move to a position in private business, perhaps after working in a public corporation. In February 2008, the same advisory panel to Prime Minister Fukuda that had previously submitted a proposal in January to reform the central bureaucracy[23] modified its initial stance on prohibiting direct contact between politicians and bureaucrats, but instead proposed that contact should be regulated and that the reforms would be implemented within five years.[24]

In March, a government advisory panel proposed the reduction of the central ministries' branch offices that are regarded as monitoring posts of the ministries. Sixty per cent of ministry officials work in the branch offices, which the ministries regard as vital to operations. But in order to downsize government and cut waste, the panel recommended that the officials be sent to prefectural or municipal government offices. Panel members from the private sector also recommended that some of the duties of central ministries be assumed by local authorities, which would encourage decentralization. However, when the Decentralization Committee met in 2007, it had expected that the ministries would submit recommendations on mergers of branch offices. The ministries did not present any positive proposals.[25]

Why can't Japan reform?

In his interview officer F expressed the prevailing sentiment among the Japanese:

> The bureaucracy controls and operates Japan. I haven't thought much about the politicians, but the bureaucracy controls everything and makes sure that things go smoothly.

Conservatism according to Koizumi and Abe: the Kishi connection

Since the late 1980s, a breed of young neo-nationalists politicians, who did not experience the war, have become a force in Japanese politics. Abe maintained in *Toward a Beautiful Country* that the Japanese are a conservative nation. Although Koizumi, whose grandfather and father were Conservative LDP politicians, was a proponent of institutional reforms,[26] he will be remembered best for his six pilgrimages to Yasukuni Shrine, where not only Japan's military dead are interned but also Class A war criminals. The Shinto shrine was founded in 1869 and run by the military until the end of the Second World War, when the United States Occupation outlawed Shintoism. Infuriated by Koizumi's apparent glorification of Japan's military past and disregard of the suffering incurred by the Chinese and Koreans during Japan's wartime occupation, China and North and South Korea lodged vehement protests. Despite angering important trading partners and Japanese pacifists, as well as businessmen whose ventures in China and South Korea were vandalized by Chinese and South Korean protestors and who were extremely concerned about the ramifications for future Japanese–Chinese economic relations, Koizumi continued his visits to the shrine, ending his term as Prime Minister with a sixth and final visit in August 2006.

Koizumi also displayed his nationalist colours by drawing up an education bill in June 2006 that for the first time revised the education bill that had been written in 1947. The new bill included the promotion of 'patriotism' as part of compulsory education, which had been mentioned in the 1947 bill. Although members of the Opposition Party voted against the bill because it might promote nationalism, the bill was passed into law in January 2007 during Abe's administration. The Basic Education Law calls, for the first time since the Second World War, for singing the national anthem and saluting the Japanese flag at school ceremonies as a part of children's education. The law also gives the education minister more power over local education boards and requires that teachers renew their licences every ten years.

On 23 May 2008 government again defied opposition to the promotion of nationalism among schoolchildren by voiding a 1949 ban on public school trips to Yasukuni Shrine. The reason given for restoring the excursions was that they would serve to educate students about Japanese culture and history.[27]

Abe, whom Koizumi had hand-picked to succeed him as prime minister, staunchly defended Koizumi's visits to Yasukuni Shrine. Abe, whose grandfather Kishi Nobuske and great uncle Sato Eisaku were post-war prime ministers and whose father was a career LDP politician, was raised from birth in an ultra-conservative milieu. Like his grandfather, Abe's political philosophy is immersed in nationalism and his administration focused on promoting bills that would serve the national interests, such as the reinstatement of the Ministry of Defence and the revision of Article 9 in the Constitution to allow Self-Defence Forces to protect Japan if Japan was attacked.

Abe maintained in *Toward a Beautiful Country* that the history reported in textbooks did not reflect a realistic picture of Japan's wartime engagement in Asia. In 2001, Abe had supported the Ministry of Education, Culture, Sports, Science and Technology's approval of a *New History Textbook* for high school students, which glosses over Japan's military expansion into Asia and the wartime atrocities committed by the Japanese military in Asia. Other proponents of the textbook included Furuya Keiji, a former senior vice-minister of METI and Ishihara Shintaru, governor of Tokyo. *Sankei Shimbun*, a conservative daily which is owned by the same ultra-conservative media group that also owns the textbook's publisher, ran a series of editorials supporting the textbook.[28] The book was written by academics who were members of the right-wing Society of Textbook Reform and who believed that Japan had entered Asia to liberate the region from the control of white colonists and that the so-called atrocities were merely 'normal excesses' committed by all armies.[29] Despite China's and South Korea's outrage over the manipulation of facts, heated debate in the national Diet and strong resistance in local govern-ments, by 2004 the book had been adopted by a minority of prefec-tures. In April 2004, the Tokyo Metropolitan board of education officially adopted the textbook, thanks to the persistence of Governor Ishihara. Later that year other prefectures such as Ehime acquiesced to government pressure (as discussed in Chapter 4).

The future: resignation and fear?

Naito told his Georgetown University audience that historically, the Japanese have relied on a higher power to govern them. This deferral to a higher power has culminated in a resigned passivism which seems to be an indelible characteristic of Japan's mono-culture. The majority of the electorate have willingly accepted guidance by a post-war governing system that has been controlled by a powerful bureaucracy, whose policies have been supported unabashedly by members of the political party that has dominated national and local politics since 1955 and by private industry.

During the last decade, the Japanese have come to understand that their 'ruling triad' administrative system has failed to solve their country's critical economic problems and growing social problems. But they also realize that it will take many years to reform a system embedded in a network of vested interests since the reformers, who have been given the responsibility to legislate structural reforms, together with their supporters are the stakeholders of the system that must be reformed. Deferral to a higher power also implies a prefer-ence for avoiding dealing with problems and allowing a higher power to find a solution. Even though the Japanese are facing exceedingly critical times, they have freely admitted that it would take another Meiji Restoration to trigger action at the grass-roots level to expedite major changes in the system.

Even if the Democratic Party of Japan were to be swept into the majority in both Houses by a rising tide of discontent among voters and even if structural reforms are initiated, the effort will be akin to plugging holes in a dyke to stem the flood of problems that are a consequence of years of reliance on an antiquated system and pork-barrel policies.

As Japan's economy continues to deteriorate and as the Japanese begin to recognize that Japan's position in the global economy is weakening, Abe's neo-nationalist philosophy is gaining popular support. A government survey conducted in April found that 43.4 per cent of the respondents saw a deterioration of the economy, an increase of 22.3 per cent from the previous year. Fifty-seven per cent of the respondents expressed a sense of patriotism and a strong love of country.[30]

The Japanese are becoming increasingly alarmed about the resurgence of nationalism and the growing influence of ultra-conservative politicians as exemplified by Tokyo's governor Ishihara Shintaru, whose racist and chauvinistic rhetoric are well-publicized by the Japanese media. His views are shared by numerous young politicians who did not experience the war. Hashimoto Toru, Osaka's governor, is an admirer.[31]

The national anthem and the flying of the Japanese flag were legally sanctioned in 1999. By 2004, even before the new education bill had been formally drawn up, teachers who refused to press students to sing the anthem and salute the flag were reprimanded. The Tokyo board of education in May of that year reprimanded 171 teachers for refusing to comply with the law. By 2007, 450 teachers had been punished by the board for non-compliance through suspension or withholding wages, resurrecting memories of the Second World War which heralded an era of Big Brother state and the intensification of government controls over society.

The government's 2008 annual report, which analyses trends in the labor force, forecast that the workforce would decrease from 66 million to 42 million, or one-third, by 2050. The government has been promoting the substitution of robots in areas such as the manufacturing sector, which would reduce the reliance on foreign workers.

Residents of foreign descent, no matter how many years they have lived in Japan, do not have the right to vote. The majority of the 600,000 Korean residents' ancestors were forced to migrate to Japan during the Japanese occupation of Korea 1910–45. Koreans have been campaigning for suffrage for years, but since 2006 have stepped up their efforts.[32] Pacifists, who are now in the minority, report that members of right-wing groups ride in black armoured vans down the streets of major metropolises spouting through loudspeakers racist oratory attacking most ethnic groups, which serves to instil a fear of foreigners and promotes paranoia about China and North Korea, especially in regards to those countries' military build-up.

The resuscitation of nationalism and anti-foreign sentiment among a growing number of Japanese may be a temporary phenomenon, but it also exposes the anxieties of the Japanese, who know that their social and economic system is deteriorating and that its stability is in jeopardy. Nevertheless, in order to ensure stable economic growth, Japan must enthusiastically cooperate and collaborate with China and the other Asian countries. However, there is the danger that a prevailing xenophobia and a mistrust of foreigners will impede the process of integration. Officer F professed:

Japan is a small island nation and insular. People are not open to outsiders. They build stoned fences and close themselves off. Japan has internationalized in some areas like trade, but for the general population, Japan has not internationalized at all.

Notes

1 Introduction

1. A. Mikuni and R. Taggart Murphy, *Japan's Policy Trap* (Washington, DC: Brookings Institution Press, 2002), p. 248.
2. S. Carpenter, *Special Corporations and the Bureaucracy: Why Japan can't reform* (Basingstoke: Palgrave Macmillan, 2003).
3. Chalmers Johnson is the only Western commentator on Japan who has written about special corporations: *Japan's Public Policy Companies* was published in 1978 (Washington, DC: AEI Press). He also wrote briefly about public corporations (he used the term 'special status companies') in connection with *amakudari* in his excellent book *JAPAN Who Governs?* (New York: W. W. Norton ,1995). He stated that public corporations extended ministerial powers, but he admitted that non-Japanese scholars had conducted little research in this area (p. 134).
4. Johnson, *JAPAN Who Governs?*, p. 15.
5. Ibid.
6. Mikuni and Murphy, *Japan's Policy Trap*, p. 39.
7. For information regarding the reform of special corporations pre-2003: Carpenter, *Special Corporations and the Bureaucracy: Why Japan can't reform*, pp. 14–50.
8. K. Iishi, *The Parasites That Are Gobbling Up Japan Dismantle All Special Corporations and Public Corporations! (Nihon wo Kuitsuku Kiseichu Tokushu Hojin Koeki Hojin wo ZenHai Seiyo!)* (Tokyo: Michi Shuppansha, 2001), p. 38.
9. *The Economist* (3 February 2008), p. 32.
10. Mikuni and Murphy, *Japan's Policy Trap*, p. 96.
11. www.OECD.org.
12. E. Lincoln, *Troubled Times* (Washington, DC: Brookings Institution, 1999), p. 190.
13. www.reuters.com (31 January 2008).
14. kyodo.co.jp (1 February 2008).
15. Mikuni and Murphy, *Japan's Policy Trap*, p. 38.
16. *Kyodo News International* (29 September 2005).
17. Ibid. (7 December 2007).
18. www.japantimes.co.jp (17 December 2005).
19. www.asahi.com (8 December 2007).
20. Ibid. (23 December 2003).
21. Ishihara's father is Ishihara Shintaru, the ultra-conservative governor of Tokyo whose nationalistic views are popular among Japanese.
22. The Ministry of Land, Infrastructure and Transport admitted on 6 February 2008 that ¥7.81 million from a special account for road tax

revenues to be used for the construction of infrastructure had been rerouted over an 18-year period through March 2007 for the purchase of massage chairs, sporting goods, mah-jong table and karaoke machines for local offices.

23. *Kyodo News International* (30 August 2003).
24. D. Pilling, FT.com (6 October 2006).
25. www.asahi.com (9 January 1995).
26. Y. Komori, *Sankei Shimbun* (13 June 1995).
27. *Sentaku* (Tokyo: July 1995), p. 86.
28. This activity commonly occurs in foreign governments' representative overseas offices.
29. W. J. Holstein, 'With Friends Like These', *U.S. New and World Report* (16 June 1997), p. 48.
30. J. McCurry, www.guardian.co.uk (1 October 2007).
31. Ibid.
32. L. Lucas, www.FT.com (14 September 2007).
33. T. Fukawa, 'Some Structural Issues in the Japanese Social Security System', *The Journal of Social Security Policy*, Vol. 4, No. 2 (Tokyo, Dec. 2005).
34. Research Institute of Economy, Trade and Industry (REITI) 'Japan's Pension System-Evaluating the 2004 Reform and Establishing Clear Principles for Further Reforms', REITI Policy Symposium (15 December 2005).
35. www.economist.com (14 June 2007).
36. Ibid.
37. www.japantimes.co.jp (9 October 2007).
38. *Kyodo News* (14 March 2008).
39. Ibid. (25 August 2001).
40. www.asahi.com (23 November 2004).
41. J. A. A. Stockwin, *Governing Japan* (London: Blackwell Publishers, 1999), p. 108.
42. www.bloomberg.com (8 February 2008).
43. *Kyodo News* (8 April 2008).
44. www.asahi.com (2 February 2008).
45. www.FT.com (31 January 2008).
46. http://home.kyodo.co.jp.
47. www.asahi.com (17 January 2008).
48. Ibid. (29 January 2008).
49. Ibid. (7 February 2008).
50. Hashimoto is an admirer of the ultra-conservative governor of Tokyo, Ishihara Shintaro.
51. www.japantimes.co.jp (7 February 2008).
52. M. Nakamoto, www.FT.com (20 December 2007).
53. www.asahi.com (20 February 2007).
54. www.yomiuri.co.jp (19 February 2008).
55. NTT is partially privatized, but government owns the holding company.
56. L. Freeman, 'Japan's Press Clubs as Information Cartels', *JPRI Working Paper No. 18*, Japan Policy Research Institute (Cardiff, CA: 1996 April).

57. A. Gamble, *A Public Betrayed* (Washington, DC: Regnery Publishing, 2004).
58. Bill Whittaker (New York, September 1994).
59. Koki Morinaga (New York, September 1994).
60. http//home.kyodo,co.jp (22 January 2007).

2   The Development of the System

1. C. Johnson, *MITI and the Japanese Miracle* (Stanford, CA: Stanford University Press, 1982), p. 24.
2. Part 2, Chapter 1 details the structure of Japan's governing system.
3. 2008 marked the 150th anniversary of signing of the trade treaty with Britain.
4. J. Sager, 'The Origins of Japan's Economic Philosophy', *JPRI Critique*, Vol. vii, No. 9, October 2000 (Cardiff, CA: Japan Policy Research Institute).
5. Ibid.
6. Ibid.
7. C. Johnson, *Japan Who Governs? The Rise of the Developmental State* (New York: W. W. Norton, 1995).
8. Idemitsu Oil, one of Japan's leading oil companies, is an example of companies that searched for fossil fuels and operated refineries in central China.
9. The Ishikawa Shipbuilding Co.'s automobile division became Isuzu Motors Co. and Kawasaki Shipbuilding Co. became Kawasaki Heavy Industries.
10. T. Okazaki, 'The Role of Holding Companies in Pre-War Japanese Economic Development', *Social Science Japan Journal*, Vol. 4, No. 2 (2001), p. 250.
11. Depression cartels are formed to limit production so that all major companies affected can continue to operate on an equal playing field.
12. Johnson (1982), p. 103 (Chapter 3 gives an exemplary chronicle of the development of Japan's industrial policy).
13. Ibid., p. 27.
14. Ibid., p. 104.
15. Ibid., pp. 109–10.
16. T. Okazaki, (2001) p. 255.
17. Non-performing loans are loans that are not currently accruing interest or on which interest is not being paid.
18. T. Nakamura, *The Postwar Japanese Economy* (Tokyo: University of Tokyo Press, 1977), p. 18.
19. A. Nakamura and Jun Hongo, www.japantimes.co.jp (10 July 2007).

3   The Elite Bureaucracy: The Image of Reform

1. R. A. Werner, *Princes of the Yen* (Armonk, NeY: M. E. harpe, 2003), p. 25.
2. The constitution is often referred to as the 'Pacifist Constitution'.

3. Johnson (1982), p. 149.
4. J. Dower, *Embracing Defeat: Japan in the Wake of World War II* (London: Penguin, 1999), p. 27.
5. The holding companies were reinstated in 1997.
6. Werner (2003), p. 131.
7. The Anti-Monopoly Law has remained relatively weak because a number of board members are MOF officials. In 1997 cross-shareholdings in the *keiretsu* was sanctioned.
8. J. A. A. Stockwin, *Governing Japan* (Blackwell, 1975), p. 105.
9. M. Negishi, www.Japantimes.co.jp (9 September 2005).
10. R. J. Samuels, 'Kishi and Corruption: An Anatomy of the 1955 System' *JPRI Working Paper*, No. 83, Japan Policy Research Institute (Cardiff, CA: December 2001).
11. T. Umehara, www.asahi.com (20 July 2006).
12. America's gold coverage in 1950 was 50 per cent.
13. K. Yamamura, 'Success That Soured: Administrative Guidance and Cartels in Japan' in K. Yamamura (ed.), *Policy and Trade Issues of the Japanese Economy* (Washington, DC: Washington University Press, 1982), p. 99.
14. Ibid.
15. A. Mikuni, 'Why Japan Can't Reform Its Economy', *JPRI Working Paper*, No. 44 Japan Policy Research Institute (Cardiff, CA: April 1998).
16. It is interesting to note that Takeo Fukuda, Yasuo Fukuda's father, became the president of the LDP in 1976 and Japan's prime minister from 1976 to 1978. He was an MOF official during the Second World War, serving as Chief Cabinet Secretary, the same post his son served in Koizumi's Cabinet. After the war, Fukuda was appointed the director of the General Accounting office. He entered politics in 1952.
17. A. Mikuni and R. Taggart Murphy (2002), p. 96.
18. A. Mikuni, 'What we should do if the U.S. economy falters', www.asahi.com (11 October 2006).
19. M. Sancheta, www.FT.com (13 March 2008).
20. Japan's fiscal year ends on 31 March.
21. M. Sancheta, www.FT.com (13 March 2008).

4   *Amakudari*: The Ties that Bind the Bureaucracy with the Private and Public Sectors and Politics

1. C. Johnson, Japan Who Governs? The Rise of the Developmental State (W. W. Norton), p. 151.
2. An appropriate example is the case of a MITI official who was loaned to JETRO's Tokyo headquarters in 1986–89. After returning to MITI for two years he was loaned to JETRO San Francisco, where he served as president for three years. While in San Francisco, he applied for and received

a Green Card. The work permit enabled him to move directly from San Francisco to JETRO New York to take the president's post for two years.

3. www.asahi.com (31 March 2007).
4. A. Hirayama and S. Sugihara, www.asahi.com (4 February 2005).
5. *Kyodo News* (23 November 2006).
6. www.japantime.com (27 August 2005).
7. Ibid. (14 October 2006).
8. K, Calder, 'Elites in an Equalizing Role: Ex-Bureaucrats as Coordinators and Intermediaries to the Japanese Government-Business Relationship', *Comparative Politics*, vol. 21, pt 4 (1989), p. 389.
9. When the author was working for a large Japanese liquor producer in Tokyo in the late 1980s, the computers used in the corporate headquarters were produced by the giant Japanese corporation NEC (Nippon Electric Company) that was established in 1899. Upon returning from holiday in 1989, the author discovered that all of the computers had been replaced with IBM computers. According to colleagues, the director of human resources had made the decision to purchase IBM PCs without consulting the president.
10. The MITI official referred to in note 2 migrated to IBM Japan after his departure from JETRO New York.
11. D. Ibison, www.FT.com (26 May 2005).
12. J. Choy, 'Japan's Non-performing Loan Problem Refuses to Go Away', *Japan Economic Institute*, 2000.
13. M. Aoki, H. Patrick and P. Sheard, 'The Japanese Main Bank System: An Introductory', in A. Aoki and H. Patrick (eds.) *The Japanese Main Bank System: Its Relevance for Developing and Transforming Economies* (Oxford: Clarence Press, 1994), p. 32.
14. Werner (2003), p. 131.
15. E. Lincoln, 'Making Some Sense of the Japanese Economy', *JPRI Working Paper*, Japan Policy Research Institute (Cardiff, CA: September 2003).
16. www.asahi.com (30 March 2005).
17. Mikuni and Murphy (2002), p. 61.
18. *Thompson Financial* (September 1999).
19. Ishihara was elected to governor in 1999. Before formally becoming politically active as a member of the LDP in 1968, he was a popular novelist whose first book, *Season of Love*, won the prestigious Akutagawa Prize. The book was a best-seller, principally because the story was about wealthy students rebelling against post-war values by engaging in gambling and promiscuous sex. The book was made into a movie. Ishihara became an idol among the Japanese, which undoubtedly aided in his bid for governor. Ishihara is a nationalist whose anti-US and anti-China stance has been well-documented in the Japanese media.
20. www.asahi.com (22 March 2008).
21. *Kyodo News* (9 March 2008).
22. www.asahi.com (19 March 2008).
23. *Kyodo News* (26 March 2008).

24. www.asahi.com (9 November 2007).
25. *Kyodo News* (21 April 2007).
26. H. Nakata, www.JapanTimes.com (25 April 2007).
27. www.asahi.com (18 April 2008).

5 Interpersonal Networks in the 'Ruling Triad'

1. K. van Wolferen, *The Enigma of Japanese Power* (Vintage Books, 1990), p. 110.
2. Assessment based on government statistics.
3. Takeshita was a member of the strongest faction in the LDP. He resigned from his post in 1989 as one of the politicians involved in the stock-for favours Recruit scandal, admitting that he had received illicit stock and cash donations from the marketing and information company.
4. At the time, local governments contributed between 20 per cent and 30 per cent of the funds for public works.
5. S. Eguchi and M. Yotsukura, www.asahi.com (7 January 2008).
6. Ibid. (12 January 2008).
7. www.asahi.com (21 June 2006).
8. Ibid. (15 June 2008).
9. www.asahi.com (30 October 2007).
10. www.FT.com (6 December 2007).
11. www.asahi.com (21 April 2008).
12. *Kyodo News* (1 December 2007).
13. J. Soble, www.FT.com (6 December 2007).
14. *Kyodo News* (29 October 2007).
15. www.asahi.com (22 December 2007).
16. Ibid.
17. Ibid. (17 November 2007).
18. *Kyodo News* (2 December 2007).
19. www.asahi.com (1 December 2007).
20. Ibid. (13 November 2007).
21. *Kyodo News* (20 January 2008).
22. www.asahi.com (21 April 2008).
23. *Kyodo News* (10 March 2008).
24. www.asahi.com (5 April 2008).
25. Ibid. (15 April 2008).
26. K. Kobayashi, *The 15-year War on Non-performing Loans and Deflation*, Research Institute of Trade and Industry (Tokyo: 2004).
27. See 'window guidance', p. 76.
28. K. Belson, *The New York Times* (19 January 2002).
29. www.asahi.com (6 December 2003).
30. Asia Times On-line (14 December 2000).
31. www.Japantimes.com (1 February 2001).
32. Ibid. (26 April 2002).
33. *Kyodo News* (27 April 2002).

34. The DBJ was known until 1999 as the Japan Development Bank (JDB), before it was merged with the bankrupt Hokkaido-Tohoku Development Finance Corporation, a MOF Special Corporation. The merger was celebrated with a new name, the Development bank of Japan (DJB).
35. K. Tsuru, 'Daiei's Rehabilitation', *Research Institute of Economy, Trade and Industry (REITI)*, 4 March 2005.
36. E. J. Lincoln, 'On Japan: Chilly Welcome', *Council On Foreign Relations* (16 February 2005).
37. D. Pilling, www.FT.com, (4 February 2004).
38. M. Sanchanta, www.FT.com (19 December 2005).
39. It is common for all of the ministries to hoard secret funds.
40. *Kyodo News* (31 January 2008).
41. Ibid. (4 April 2008).

6   The Elite Bureaucracy: Prisoners of the System

1. Johnson (1995).
2. While the author was working in Tokyo for a large liquor and pharma-ceutical producer during the late 1980s, she had the opportunity to meet staff from the major trading companies and MITI and share perspectives about the Uruguay Rounds and the General Agreement on Tariffs and Trade (GATT). Although the author had intended to apply for work related to promoting America's trade policies, ideally with the USTR, she began to reassess the objectives of US trade policies with Japan. America's trade policies with Japan were significantly influenced by America's interests in the Pacific and the need to ensure Japan's commitment as America's conservative and cooperative ally in the region. But these interests also served to preserve a system of administration of Japan's political economy that was no longer able to cope with the serious prob-lems connected to the asset-inflated bubble of the 1980s. At the end of the Cold War in 1989, many Japanese were concerned that the United States would take a tougher stand in trade negotiations because it would no longer be dependent on Japan in the Pacific.

   The author decided to seek employment with Japanese organizations upon returning to the United States. Work at JETRO New York provided the opportunity to observe not only METI officials, but also officers who represented prefecture governments and a number of other ministries' Special Corporations, such as the Japan Highway Corporation. The office was a microcosm of Japanese government agencies whose officials were sent to the United States specifically to assess business opportunities for Japanese firms and American markets for Japanese products. There were approximately 40 officials on loan to the JETRO office.
3. K. Tsutsumi, *The Monster Ministries and Amakudari: White Paper on Corruption* (Kodansha, 2000), pp. 144–75.
4. Tsutsumi is currently a journalist.

5. During governor Iga's administration, Iyo Bank, Ehime's main bank, operated a one-man representative office in the Manhattan World Trade Center
and in London. They were closed at the end of Iga's administration.

7 The Interviews

1. The officer's duties as the director of the import division encompassed the
Foreign Access Zones. Governor Iga had established close relationships
with ministry officials, namely from MITI and the Ministry of
Construction, whom he entertained extensively. Among them was the
president of JETRO New York. Iga's son opened the first Ehime desk in
JETRO New York during the president's tenure and stayed from 1992–94.
His responsibilities focused on entertaining delegations of businessmen
from his region. He and the MITI official were on friendly terms. When
Iga's son returned to Ehime, he became the director of Ehime's Foreign
Access Zone, the first Foreign Access Zone to open in Japan. The Ehime desk
continued until the end of Iga's administration, when it was closed. An
Ehime representative desk was subsequently set up at JETRO Hong Kong.
2. In Chapter 4, p. 71, it was explained that elite officials who are not considered for further promotion may be posted in a Special Corporation
until they retire.
3. The officer's successor was a native of the prefecture. He was 35. His family
were farmers and he was the first member to graduate from a university.
His first childhood impressions about the United States were influenced
by the stories his grandmother told him about the American B-29 bombers
that flew over their home during the war. When he arrived in New York,
he rented a home in an upper-middle-class suburb, one hour commute
from Manhattan, where his young daughter could attend a private school.
The home had a large swimming and a garden. The officer's wife, who was
eight-months pregnant with their second child, joined her husband a
month later. A year after their second daughter's birth, the child fell into
the swimming pool while unattended. She was rescued, but emergency
services were called to resuscitate her and take her by air ambulance to a
hospital. The unfortunate accident left the daughter mentally and physically incapacitated and she remained in hospital a number of weeks. Since
the daughter was born in the United States, she was eligible for Medicare
and received excellent and compassionate care, which included continuing physical therapy after she returned home. Nevertheless, the officer
and his wife knew that upon their return to Japan, they would be held
responsible for the accident.
   The officer arranged a large exhibition for old and well-established
small businesses engaged in traditional industries in his prefecture in
order to introduce their products to New Yorkers, with the expectation
that there was a market for their products in the United States. Some of
the firms had been in operation since the eighteenth century. Although

partially subsidized by government, the tradesmen assumed the sizable portion of the costs of shipping their wares to New York and setting up exhibition stalls. Some of the owners had never travelled to the United States and did not speak English and were exhausted from the effort. The exhibition continued for three days and many Americans enjoyed their first exposure to the elegant products presented to them. At the end of the last day, the officer spoke at length to the firms' owners about the viability of their products in the American market place. He characterized American consumers as couch potatoes who sat all day watching television while eating spaghetti out of cans and drinking quantities of beer. His analysis did not include other market information that may have given the tradesmen more positive perspectives.

4. Mishima (1925–1970) was nominated for the Nobel Prize for Literature three times. He is considered one of the greatest writers of the twentieth century because of his vast vocabulary and flawless use of Chinese characters. He was born into a family of bureaucrats and was a nationalist. He enlisted in the Ground Defence Force in 1962. In the same year, Mishima formed a private army of which most of the members were students and pledged to protect the emperor, whom he felt exemplified the Japanese spirit. On 25 November 1970 Mishima, accompanied by four members of his army, tried to instigate a *coup d'état* at the Self-Defence Force headquarters in Tokyo. They broke into the Commandant's room and held the commander hostage. When Mishima read his manifesto to the soldiers who had congregated below, he was jeered. Humiliated, Mishima returned to the room and committed suicide.

5. Ishihara was a friend of Mishima. His book *The Japanese Can Say No (No to Ieru Nihon)* was a collaborative effort with the late Akio Morita, Sony founder and chairman, published in 1989 and was a best-seller. Ishihara argued in the book that the United States regarded Japan as a subordinate and that this attitude was related to racism. Ishihara's initial exposure to the United States was during the war when his neighbourhood was strafed by American aircraft. Ishihara claimed that the aircraft flew so low that he could see the pictures of naked women and cartoon characters painted on the sides of the planes.

6. White Anglo-Saxon Protestants (WASP) was originally a term used to refer to white Americans whose ancestors were white Protestants who had immigrated to America from Europe. Although the term refers to an upper-class, white, wealthy elite like Rockfeller or Carnegie, the Japanese use it to describe all Americans who are Christians and white like the Kennedy family, who are Catholics.

7. The officer is referring to an Executive Order issued by President Kennedy in March 1961 that required businesses that received government funding for projects to give equal treatment to job applicants and employees regardless of race, gender or ethnicity. The initial action provided the framework for the initiation of anti-discriminatory laws that were intended to promote equal representation of minorities and women in education, businesses and the public sector.

8. During the year that the author worked as newsroom manager for the North American branch of Japan's leading commercial news station during the first Gulf War, she saw that coverage about America by Japanese media and reporting on Japan by American media could often be a manipulation of facts. The Japanese journalists in the station reported on political and international issues, but also, at the frequent request of the Tokyo headquarters, searched specifically for stories on crime, drugs and abortion issues. When former President George Bush was scheduled to speak at the fiftieth anniversary of Pearl Harbor, the journalists were asked to investigate reports that American soldiers had perpetuated atrocities against Iraqi soldiers.

The American press countered with extensive coverage of sexual harassment in Japanese corporate operations in the United States, Japanese military atrocities committed during the Second World War, 'comfort-women', and so-forth.

8 Conclusion

1. www.asahi.com (14 may 2008).
2. S. Carpenter, *Special Corporations and the Bureaucracy: Why Japan Can't Reform* (Basingstoke: Palgrave Macmillan, 2003), p. 121.
3. *Kyodo News* (13 February 2008).
4. A level below 50 registers pessimism.
5. www.kyodo.com (18 April).
6. Ibid.
7. Reuters in Tokyo (15 February 2008).
8. *Kyodo News* (9 April 2008).
9. www.bloomberg.com (15 February 2008).
10 Forbes (23 November 2007).
11. Reuters (13 February 2008).
12. www.asahi.com (11 April 2008).
13. AFP (15 May 2008).
14. *Kyodo News* (20 May 2008).
15. Ibid. (28 May 2008).
16. Ibid. (7 April 2008).
17. Ibid. (14 March 2008).
18. Ibid. (26 February 2008).
19. M. Nakamoto, www.Ft.com (5 March 2008).
20. Ibid. (22 April 2008).
21. Due to pressure from the United States, Japan began to open the domestic market to foreign rice in the late 1980s. Despite the aura of liberalization, Japanese rice is aggressively protected by government and Japanese rice farmers are supported through direct and indirect subsidies distributed through various government programmes.
22. *Kyodo News* (14 April 2008).
23. See p. 99.

24. www.asahi.com (1 February 2008).
25. www.asahi.com (1 March 2008).
26. Koizumi's Cabinet State Minister of Administrative and Regulatory Reform in 2002 was Ishihara Nobuteru, the son of Tokyo governor Ishihara Shintaru.
27. *Kyodo News* (23 May 2008).
28. D. McNeill, 'History Redux: Japan's Textbook Battle Reignites', *JPRI Working Paper*, No. 107, Japan Policy Research Institute (Cardiff, CA: June 2005).
29. Ibid.
30. *Kyodo News* (12 April 2008).
31. Hashimoto proposed in April 2008 that 36 native English teachers belonging to the Native English Teachers Programme be replaced by Japanese English teachers in order to cut spending. The teachers were offered short-term, four-month contracts from April–July.
32. Ibid. (18 April 2008).

Select Bibliography

Aoki, M., Patrick H., and Sheard, P., 'The Japanese Main Bank System: An Introductory', in M. Aoki and H. Patrick (eds), *The Japanese Main Bank System: Its Relevance for Developing and Transforming Economies* (Oxford: Clarence Press, 1994).

Calder, K., 'Elites in an Equalizing Role: Ex-Bureaucrats as Coordinators and Intermediaries in the Japanese Government Relationship', *Comparative Politics*, vol. 21, pt 4 (New York: 1989 July), pp.379–403.

Carpenter, S., *Special Corporations and the Bureaucracy: Why Japan Can't Reform* (Basingstoke: Palgrave Macmillan, 2003).

Choy, J., 'Japan's Non-Performing Loan Problem Refuses to Go Away', *Japan Economic Institute* (2000).

Dower, J., *Embracing Defeat: Japan in the Wake of World War II* (London: Penguin, 1999).

Freeman, L., 'Japan's Press Clubs as Information Cartels', *JPRI Working Paper*, No. 18, Japan Policy Research Institute (Cardiff, CA: 1996 April).

Furukawa, T., 'Some Structural Issues in the Japanese Social Security System', *The Journal of Social Security Policy*, vol. 4, no. 2 (Tokyo: 2005 December).

Gamble, A., *A Public Betrayed* (Washington, DC: Regney Publishing, 2004).

Iishi, K., *The Parasites That Are Gobbling Up Japan: Dismantle All Special Corporations and Public Corporations! [Nihon wo Kuitsuku Kiseichu: Tokushu Hojin Koeiki Hojin wo Zenhai Seiyo!]* (Tokyo: Michi Shuppansha, 1999).

Johnson, C., 'The Reemployment of Retired Government Bureaucrats in Japanese Big Business', *Asian Survey*, vol. 14, no. 11 (Berkeley, CA: University of California Press, Nov. 1974), pp. 953–65.

Johnson. C., *MITI and the Japanese Miracle* (Stanford, CA: Stanford University Press, 1982).

Johnson, C., *JAPAN Who Governs?* (New York: W. W. Norton, 1995).

Kobayashi, K., *The 15-Year War on Non-Performing Loans and Deflation*, Research Institute of Trade and Industry (Tokyo, 2004).

Lincoln, E., *Troubled Times* (Washington, DC: Brookings Institution Press, 1999).

Lincoln, E., 'Making Some Sense of the Japanese Economy', *JPRI Working Paper*, No. 94, Japan Policy Research Institute (Cardiff, CA: 2003 September).

Lincoln, E., 'On Japan: Chilly Welcome', *Council on Foreign Relations* (16 February 2005).

McNeill, D., 'History Redux: Japan's Textbook Battle Reignites', *JPRI Working Paper*, No. 107, Japan Policy Research Institute (Cardiff, CA 2005 September).

Mikuni, A., 'Why Japan Can't Reform Its Economy', *JPRI Working Paper*, No. 44, Japan Policy Research Institute (1998 April).

Mikuni, A. and Murphy, R. T., *Japan's Policy Trap* (Washington, DC: Brookings Institution Press, 2002).

Nakamura, T., *The Postwar Japanese Economy* (Tokyo: University of Tokyo Press, 1977).

Okazaki, T., 'The Role of Holding Companies in Pre-War Japanese Economic Development', *Social Science Japan Journal*, vol. 4, no. 2 (2001), pp. 243–68.

Porter, Michael E., Hirotaka Takeuchi and Mariko Sakakibara, *Can Japan Compete?* (Basingstoke: Palgrave Macmillan, 2000).

Samuels, R., 'Kishi and Corruption: An Anatomy of the 1955 System', *JPRI Working Paper*, No. 83, Japan Policy Research Institute (Cardiff, CA: 2001 December).

Stockwin, J. A. A., *Governing Japan* (London: Blackwell Publishers, 1999).

Tsuru, K., 'Daiei's Rehabilitation', *Research Institute of Economy* (4 March 2005).

Tsutsumi, K., *The Monster Ministries and Amakudari: White Paper on Corruption* [*Kyodai Shocho Amakudari: fuhai hakusho*] (Tokyo: Kodansha, 2000).

Van Wolferen, K., *The Enigma of Power* (New York: Vintage Books, 1990).

Werner, R., *Princes of the Yen* (Armonk, NY: M. E. Sharpe, 2003).

Yamamura, K., 'Success That Soured: Administrative Guidance and Cartels in Japan', in K. Yamamura (ed.), *Policy and Trade Issues of the Japanese Economy* (Washington: Washington University Press, 1982).

Index